Cambridge Elements

Elements in Cognitive Linguistics
edited by
Sarah Duffy
Northumbria University
Nick Riches
Newcastle University

COLOUR CONCEPTS FROM A LINGUISTIC AND LITERARY PERSPECTIVE

Kimberley Pager-McClymont
University of Aberdeen's International Study Centre

Suzanne McClure
University of Liverpool

Amélie Doche
Birmingham City University

Shaftesbury Road, Cambridge CB2 8EA, United Kingdom

One Liberty Plaza, 20th Floor, New York, NY 10006, USA

477 Williamstown Road, Port Melbourne, VIC 3207, Australia

314–321, 3rd Floor, Plot 3, Splendor Forum, Jasola District Centre, New Delhi – 110025, India

103 Penang Road, #05–06/07, Visioncrest Commercial, Singapore 238467

Cambridge University Press is part of Cambridge University Press & Assessment, a department of the University of Cambridge.

We share the University's mission to contribute to society through the pursuit of education, learning and research at the highest international levels of excellence.

www.cambridge.org
Information on this title: www.cambridge.org/9781009511353

DOI: 10.1017/9781009511377

© Kimberley Pager-McClymont, Suzanne McClure and Amélie Doche 2026

This publication is in copyright. Subject to statutory exception and to the provisions of relevant collective licensing agreements, no reproduction of any part may take place without the written permission of Cambridge University Press & Assessment.

When citing this work, please include a reference to the DOI 10.1017/9781009511377

First published 2026

A catalogue record for this publication is available from the British Library

A Cataloging-in-Publication data record for this Element is available from the Library of Congress

ISBN 978-1-009-51136-0 Hardback
ISBN 978-1-009-51135-3 Paperback
ISSN 2633-3325 (online)
ISSN 2633-3317 (print)

Cambridge University Press & Assessment has no responsibility for the persistence or accuracy of URLs for external or third-party internet websites referred to in this publication and does not guarantee that any content on such websites is, or will remain, accurate or appropriate.

For EU product safety concerns, contact us at Calle de José Abascal, 56, 1°, 28003 Madrid, Spain, or email eugpsr@cambridge.org

Colour Concepts from a Linguistic and Literary Perspective

Elements in Cognitive Linguistics

DOI: 10.1017/9781009511377
First published online: January 2026

Kimberley Pager-McClymont
University of Aberdeen's International Study Centre

Suzanne McClure
University of Liverpool

Amélie Doche
Birmingham City University

Author for correspondence: Kimberley Pager-McClymont,
mcclymont@abdn.ac.uk

Abstract: This Element adopts a holistic approach to the processing of colours in language and literature, weaving together insights from cognitive linguistics, psychology, and literary studies. Through diverse case studies, it underpins the symbolic power of colours in evoking characters' emotional states, moral traits, and cultural perceptions (Section 2). Section 3 explores how colour metaphors such as DISCOMFORT IS BROWN influence readers' cognitive and emotional responses, drawing on psychology research on colour–emotion association. Section 4 examines how the lexeme *colourless* functions as its own oxymoron and is used figuratively through the metaphor ANATOMY IS MIND in Modernist literature. Each section draws on cognitive linguistic tools, showcasing how colours shape not just visual but emotional engagement with texts. By connecting cognitive science, psychology, and literary analysis, this Element offers an interdisciplinary perspective, demonstrating that colours act as stimuli shaping perception, language, and cultural meaning, enriching the literary experience across contexts and cultures.

Keywords: colours, stylistics, corpora, psychology, metaphor

© Kimberley Pager-McClymont, Suzanne McClure and Amélie Doche 2026

ISBNs: 9781009511360 (HB), 9781009511353 (PB), 9781009511377 (OC)
ISSNs: 2633-3325 (online), 2633-3317 (print)

Contents

1 Introduction   1

2 Colour Concepts: From Verbal to Cognitive Processes   3

3 Colour Concepts, Metaphor, and Psychology   12

4 Absence of Colour Concepts: *Colourlessness* in Literary Prose   26

5 Concluding Remarks   45

References   48

1 Introduction

There is long-standing fascination with the study of colour among scholars from linguistics, psychology, art, and cognitive science. Scholars from various fields, including linguistics, psychology, art, and cognitive science, have long been fascinated by the study of colour. However, the cognitive and emotional significance of colour use, particularly in the context of literature and language, has not been fully explored. In this Element, we aim to address this gap by examining the relationship between language, emotion, and colours through a comprehensive approach that integrates cognitive linguistics, literary analysis, psychology, and corpus linguistics. As such, we propose the following research questions:

1. How are colour concepts utilised in language and literature?
2. How are colour concepts employed symbolically in literature, and what cognitive or emotional effects do these symbolic uses have on readers?
3. How is the absence of colour in literature perceived by readers?

To answer these research questions, this Element takes an interdisciplinary approach, linking cognitive science, psychology, and literary studies to reveal how colours shape thought, emotion, and literary expression. It is organised into three main sections, each offering distinct insights that together advance the Element's central aims.

Section 2 explores how languages across cultures identify and categorise colours, revealing near-universal patterns in colour hierarchies. It establishes that colour terms are deeply rooted in metaphorical expressions and carry strong emotional connotations across languages, providing a foundation for the linguistic exploration of colour concepts. It explores how certain colours are tied to universal cognitive processes that transcend cultural boundaries, while others are more culturally specific. In addition, this section examines how, in literary fiction, authors draw on cultural colour symbolism to depict characters' inner emotional states, as well as their moral qualities and flaws, which has the potential to reinforce these traits schematically in readers' minds. This section highlights how specific colours act as symbolic markers in literature, guiding readers' emotional and conceptual engagement with characters.

Section 3 links metaphor and psychology. Using Pager-McClymont's model of pathetic fallacy (2021a, 2021b, 2022, 2023), it examines how this literary technique maps emotional experiences to colourful environmental descriptions. By integrating findings from psychology on colour and emotion with literary analysis of pathetic fallacy, this research reveals a clear correspondence between scientific and literary representations of mood. Going beyond general links between psychology and language, this section highlights how textual uses of colour reveal experiences of discomfort and uneasiness, with bottom-up mappings of DISCOMFORT IS BROWN and UNEASINESS IS GREY. The contributions of this section lie in its interdisciplinary approach, highlighting how colour can influence readers' emotional responses and exploring the potential of creative metaphors to enrich understanding and engagement.

Section 4 delves into the often-overlooked concept of *colourlessness* or absence of colours and its impact on perception, using Modernist literature (*The Modernist Literature Project* Corpus) as a case study. Utilising corpus linguistics, this section uncovers how colourless descriptors are used figuratively to evoke mood, tone, and emotional detachment, revealing that the absence of colour is as meaningful as its presence. The findings convey that *colourless* is predominantly used negatively in Modernist texts, often to describe characters and their surroundings. This finding is notable for showing the cognitive and emotional significance of 'non-colours', offering insight into the ways readers may respond to and interpret literary texts.

Each section contributes a unique perspective, showing that colours are more than mere visual stimuli – they play a central role in cognitive and emotional processing and are key components of language and literary expression. By combining literary criticism with cognitive linguistics and psychological research, this Element provides a focussed interdisciplinary analysis of colour, illuminating how humans perceive, conceptualise, and interpret colours specifically within language and literature.

This Element is transformative in its approach because it investigates colour concepts across multiple fields – literary studies, psychology, and corpus linguistics – while consistently employing cognitive linguistics as the central analytical framework. This Element considers how colours function as more than decorative details, suggesting that they may influence readers' mental representations of scenes, characters, surroundings, and events – a connection explored in depth through the analyses in subsequent sections. By drawing on multiple disciplines, this research provides a more nuanced understanding of colour in literature, with insights from each field integrated and interpreted through cognitive linguistic frameworks. For example, research in psychology has shown that certain colours tend to evoke specific emotional responses, providing empirical context for our literary analysis. The research findings presented in this

Element go beyond mere description by employing cognitive linguistics to show that colour concepts influence how readers mentally construct and engage with texts.

To clarify the systematic approach underlying this Element, each section applies complementary methods – literary analysis, cognitive linguistics, corpus linguistics, and psychology – in a coordinated framework. Literary analysis identifies patterns of colour usage and symbolic functions, cognitive linguistics maps conceptual associations, psychological studies illuminate emotional and perceptual responses, and corpus linguistics provides empirical support across texts. By integrating these approaches, the Element ensures that insights from one field inform and reinforce those from another, creating a coherent methodology for examining how colour shapes both the structure of literary texts and readers' cognitive and emotional engagement. This framework also offers a replicable model for future research, demonstrating how interdisciplinary analysis can be systematic, cumulative, and adaptable to other aspects of literary study.

2 Colour Concepts: From Verbal to Cognitive Processes

This section lays the linguistic and cultural groundwork by showing how colour concepts can activate schemas and conceptual mappings, preparing the way for the psychological and metaphorical analyses of Section 3. This section is organised as a cline that moves from the linguistic categorisation of colours to their interpretive potential in literary texts, foregrounding the cognitive linguistic perspective that meaning arises through conceptual structures and schemas. It begins with the language of colour, examining colour lexemes, their semantic ranges, and idiomatic expressions, while also attending to the cross-cultural variation that demonstrates how different communities segment and label the colour spectrum. From this foundation, the section turns to the cognitive and cultural associations between colour and emotion, showing how affective meanings are not inherent properties of colours but emerge through entrenched conceptual mappings and cultural models. The final section focusses on literature as a domain in which colour lexemes extend beyond their descriptive function to operate symbolically, which can activate, reshape, or even challenge established schemas. Drawing on cognitive linguistic frameworks such as Schema Theory and Conceptual Metaphor Theory, this section emphasises how colour meanings are constructed through conceptual mappings, cultural models, and schema activation, demonstrating that colour lexemes are not fixed labels but dynamic resources for meaning-making. In this way, the section progresses from analysing colour as a matter of meaning, to understanding it as a vehicle of perception and emotional resonance, and finally to interpreting it as a literary and cultural resource with the power to complicate or transform established ways of seeing.

2.1 The Language of Colours

Scholarly approaches to the examination of the linguistic and literary realisation of colour in literary discourse are addressed in this Element. Beyond the myriad of terms that identify primary (red, yellow, and blue) and secondary colours, there are semantically related words such as *bright* and *luminous*, which also possess significance in modern languages. The origin of the naming of colours across distinct and diverse cultures occurred in similar order: black, white, red, green, yellow, and blue (Dedrick, 1998; Biggam and Kay, 2006; Biggam et al., 2011; Loretto et al., 2012; Kaskatayeva et al., 2020). The colour spectrum pervades not just the modern lexica and the visual world but also our emotions, perceptions, and cognition.

Colours and related terms are often found in linguistic devices such as idiomatic and conceptual metaphors – although the latter, as we argue in this section, are not merely linguistic devices. Idioms containing colour concepts are widely used in spoken discourse, often carrying strong positive or negative evaluations. These linguistic constructions allow one concept to be transferred or mapped onto another so that we can be *tickled pink* when happy or *green with envy* when jealous. The emotional associations generated by colour concepts and descriptors vary amongst spoken languages and are rooted in native cultures (Hupka et al., 1997). In contrast to English, Germans would be *yellow with envy* (gelb von Neid) and if they had too much to drink they would *be blue* (blau sein). Some colour-related idiomatic expressions are the same across language, but colour descriptors often have varying connotations across cultures, and it is key to acknowledge that there are nuances in cultural colour perception. For example, in French the idiomatic phrase to express rage is *être vert de rage* (to be green with rage) whereas in English rage is associated with red. Similarly, *avoir une peur bleue* (to have a blue fear) associates blue and fear. In English blue tends to represent sadness (to feel blue) or feature more colloquial risqué ideas such as to tell blue jokes. This illustrates the varied linguistic and cultural associations of colour in discourse and it demonstrates how deeply intertwined colours are with emotion, reflecting both universal patterns and culturally specific nuances across languages.[1]

2.2 Colours, Cognition, and Emotions

Colours are an inherent part of our surroundings and impact how we view the world – though it is worth pointing out that colour perception can vary amongst individual (i.e., turquoise is often debated to be green or blue) and some individuals do not perceive colours due any level of blindness. Nevertheless, colours are frequently used to express emotions as discussed earlier, or to express other abstract concepts (i.e., something unexpected is *out of the blue*, something uncertain is a 'grey area', or being unaware of something is to be *in the dark*). The association of colours with emotions can be cultural and/or social. When colours and emotions occur in tandem, the focus is on the abstract symbolism of the colour rather than on any – and perhaps more concrete – visual or linguistic characteristics (Jonauskaite et al., 2020a: 18; see also Hupka et al., 1997; Wang et al., 2014). For example, in the United Kingdom, the colour white is worn by a bride, whereas in India it is the colour of mourning and brides wear red.

For cognitive stylisticians, style is not primarily a linguistic phenomenon but, rather, a social and ideological one. Hence, the persistent matching of one colour (e.g., red) with one emotion (e.g., anger) can help to build a schema (e.g., 'red equals anger', see Hupka et al., 1997). In such instances, the correspondence between a given colour and its corresponding emotion is conceptual in the sense that it reflects the ways in which we interpret the world. Palmer and Schloss (2010) show that people easily link colours with emotions and many of these associations are analogous across cultures. There is a high-level of cross-cultural similarities between colour and emotion perceptions, and close geographic and strong linguistic connections between languages produce similar levels of association (Jonauskaite et al., 2020a). The effect that context and culture have on mental states and emotions in colour-related expressions is significant as the interpretation, perception, and connotation can vary cross-culturally. Through online surveys, Jonauskaite et al. (2019) investigate colour–emotion pairings amongst 711 native English, German, Chinese, and Greek speakers. Participants were asked questions concerning 12 colour terms

---

[1] It is worth noting that whilst we acknowledge that there is cultural variability of colour perception, we are of French and American background living in the UK, thus using our context in the examples we focus on.

and 20 discrete emotions, resulting in 240 colour–emotion pairs. The researchers concluded that variances in the results could be partially attributed to different colour metaphors that exist in the native language and their resulting interpreted meaning. Colours may generate different associations because of the schema (or mental construal) that is produced. As mentioned previously, the idiom *green with envy* is part of the English-speaking culture. In Russian, there are two options: to be *white with envy* if they are feeling compassionate or *black with envy* when expressing negative or spiteful emotions. The mental representation of colour varies across languages, as there is no globally acknowledged schema for specific emotions. Research by Jonauskaite et al. (2020b) on colour–emotion associations suggests there is a human universal basis, but no associations are shared at 100%, thus also highlighting the subjective and unique processing of emotions.

The correspondence between colours and emotions can thus be metaphorical, allowing individuals to draw on shared concepts (colours) to convey a more personal or subjective concept (emotions). This aligns with Lakoff and Johnson (1980: 153) who argue that 'metaphor is primarily a matter of thought and action and only derivatively a matter of language'. This implies that although metaphors are usually considered thought processes, they primarily frame our perception of the world by associating concepts with one another. During the reading process, the use of colours to describe elements of a scene such as a room, an item or even a character, contributes to readers' mental representation of the scene. In fact, depending on readers' personal and subjective experience and the culture or society in which they live, their favouring of one colour over another might impact their views of the scene being read. Although the positive and negative association of colours is cultural, personal and thus subjective, there is a consensus amongst cognitive researchers that certain colours are typically associated with specific concepts across cultures and languages. Particularly in the field of metaphor research, positive emotions are typically associated with the idea of *light* (a bright day), and negative emotions with *darkness* (dark thoughts) (Arnheim, 1969; Lakoff and Johnson, 1980; Meier and Robinson, 2005; Forceville and Renckens, 2013). This is in agreement with anthropologists Berlin and Kay (1969; see also Kay et al., 1991) who argue that there is a categorisation of colours across languages, the main two being black which is often seen as negative and white often being seen as positive.

This contrast is also prevalent in literature, particularly in the representation of key events or characters, where colour choices can contribute to the activation of underlying schemas and guide readers' interpretations. For example, in Brontë's Wuthering Heights (1847/2021), Cathy's two love interests Heathcliff and Edgar are portrayed as opposite of each other (Le Fanu, 2003; Imsallim, 2014). Heathcliff is tumultuous and described with dark attributes as shown in the passages: 'he little imagined how my heart warmed towards him when I beheld his *black* eyes withdraw so suspiciously under their brows'; and 'he is a *dark-skinned* gipsy in aspect, in dress and manners a gentleman'). On the other hand, Edgar is calm and devoted to Cathy. He is described with light and fair attributes, which is a source of jealousy for Heathcliff. This is expressed in the sentences: 'I must wish for Edgar Linton's great *blue* eye', and 'I wish I had *light hair and a fair skin*, and was dressed and behaved as well'. The two men's opposite personality traits are reflected in their physical appearances: Heathcliff is portrayed negatively through darker attributes, and Edgar is represented positively with lighter traits. Although not a Black man, Heathcliff is racialised and treated as a member of a lower class (Soberano, 2023: 147; Althubaiti, 2015: 202) – hence the term 'gipsy boy' to describe him. Throughout the novel, the use of those colourful oppositions extends to Cathy's relationship with the two men.

These juxtaposed colour tones are at times symbolic and unique to a particular narrative or attributed with broader conceptual significance in the overall storyline. Such symbolism illustrates how colour in literature is more than descriptive: it participates in meaning-making by cueing readers to interpretive patterns and narrative schemas. Colours are often used in literature not just to describe, but also to evoke conceptual and emotional responses (see Section 3), reflecting cultural models and guiding the activation of schematic knowledge. Section 2.3 demonstrates how powerful and symbolic colours can be in the varied literary examples discussed, highlighting their role in structuring readers' understanding and extending beyond literal representation.

2.3 Colours, Schemas, and Literature

Drawing on the principles of Systemic Functional Linguistics (SFL), we conceptualise meaning-making as occurring along a continuum, with culture (the generalised, shared systems of meaning) at one end, and individual interpretation (the particular) at the other (Martin and White, 2005: 25). Literature occupies a central position on this spectrum, functioning as a semiotic artefact that draws on culturally embedded meanings while simultaneously inviting diverse individual responses. As Butt and Lukin (2009: 214) observe, 'textual organisation is *metonymic* (our emphasis) with respect to complex cultural configurations which may be, or may not be, explicitly encoded elsewhere in the culture'. In this sense, literature may be understood as offering partial, indirect representations of cultural knowledge. This dynamic interplay between cultural resources and individual interpretation is further illuminated by Schema Theory, which posits that a reader's engagement with a text is shaped by pre-existing cognitive structures and conceptual knowledge – that is, schemas. These schemas, comprising socially acquired background knowledge, are continuously 'reinforced' or 'challenged' in the act of reading (Cook, 1990: 244). Like SFL, Schema Theory foregrounds the dialectical relationship between individual cognition and broader socio-cultural semiotics: schemas are shaped by culture and enacted by individuals, just as linguistic choices in texts are both socially patterned and personally interpreted. In stylistic analysis, schemas thus serve as 'skeletal frameworks' of conceptual knowledge that help explain how readers process and interpret literary texts (Wales, 2011: 376; see also Bartlett, 1995), offering a valuable complement to SFL's concern with the cultural patterning of language. This section explores the metonymic potential of colour representation in literature through examples from American and French texts. Drawing on Schema Theory and SFL, we adopt a bottom-up analytical approach: we first examine how colours function within the immediate textual environment before situating their meanings within broader cultural and ideational schemas. The aim is to demonstrate how the language of colours can shape not just meaning, but also mental representation of a scene or textual element beyond the colour itself.

Our first example is Alice Walker's epistolary novel *The Color Purple* (1982). In this context, Celie's longing for a purple dress reflects her association of the colour purple with royalty (Krafts et al., 2011: 9). However, in Letter 12 near the end of the novel, Shug (Celie's friend and love interest) states, 'I think it pisses God off if you walk by *the color purple* in a field somewhere and don't notice it'. In this instance, the colour purple emphasises the importance of small pleasures in life, which Celie has had too little of because of the hardship and abuse she has experienced (Wu and Wei, 2022; Anwer, 2023). Four years before the publication of the novel, over 100,000 women donning shades of purple marched in Washington, D.C. for the Equal Rights Amendment (Bennetts, 1978). Since then, in America, purple has come to represent women's strength and resilience against various forms of sexual, verbal, and political abuse and neglect. In

The Color Purple, the colour purple may not, on its own, prompt readers to fully activate a ROYALTY or ABUSE schema, but American readers familiar with or particularly attuned to domestic abuse may draw on their contextual knowledge to activate this latent schema. Indeed, in today's America, the colour purple is used every October in campaigns and advertisements for Domestic Violence Awareness Month. Should the reader activate this schema via textual cues, then it will become reinforced.

In certain literary narratives, colours are repeated, creating a link between characters in addition to being a leitmotif. Such an example can be observed in Flaubert's Madame Bovary (1857/2021), in which Emma Bovary, a daydreamer often lost in her fantasies, has an affair with a younger man named Leon. The colour blue is omnipresent and there are fifty-six occurrences in the novel, reminding readers that Emma tends to have her 'head in the sky' as well as it being the colour of Leon's eyes (Tipper, 1989: 105). Furthermore, both characters are often described as wearing blue clothing when together; there are numerous items of décor, such as curtains or vases, that are also blue. Examples from the story include: 'his legs, in *blue* stockings', 'this letter, sealed with a small seal in *blue* wax', 'in post chaises behind *blue* silken curtains', 'she wanted for her mantelpiece two large *blue* glass vases', and 'she wore a small *blue* silk necktie'. The omnipresence of the colour blue in *Madame Bovary* represents the relationship between Emma and Leon and its significance for Emma. Specifically, it symbolises Emma's aspiration towards the absolute or, put more simply, her dreams (Knapp, 1980: 13). In this respect, the schema of the prototypical French reader can become reinforced since blue explicitly symbolises liberty and freedom in the French flag (Tipper, 1989: 106; Joao Cordeiro, 2015: 213). For the two French authors of this element, the link between blue and FREEDOM gets very quickly activated upon their reading of *Madame Bovary*. While non-French readers may not activate the same schema, blue tends to generally represent possibility and infinity – a schema that many narratives activate. In Kate Chopin's *The Awakening*, for instance, the colour blue – associated with the sea in that novel – represents Edna Pontellier's fantasised life breaking from gendered duties, much like Emma Bovary. These examples illustrate Wales's argument (2011: 277) that colours function as leitmotifs in Western literature.

In other narratives, colours are used to convey an implicit message to readers, acting as a more abstract leitmotif. This is the case for Melville's *Moby Dick* (1851/1988), in which scholars interpret the whiteness of the sperm whale as Ahab's search for spirituality, since white is often associated with Christianity (Stoll, 1951; Redden, 2011). In chapter 42 of the novel, entitled 'The Whiteness of the Whale', Melville (1851/1988: 212) writes:

> *Whiteness* is not so much a color as the visible absence of color, and at the same time the concrete of all colors: it is for these reasons that there is such a dumb blankness, full of meaning, in the wide landscape of snows – a colorless, all color of atheism which we shrink.

This passage features the lexical field of whiteness ('snows', 'absence of color', 'blankness', and 'colorless' – for a discussion on *colourless*, see Section 4). This demonstrates how important the use of the colour white is throughout the novel. It also illustrates the significance of the choice of colour for the whale and what it means for Ahab's chase: white is the absence of colour, mirroring Ahab's deprivation of faith as shown by the phrase 'color of atheism' in the earlier passage (Callahan, 2003). Interestingly, Melville plays with the meaning potential inscribed in the American nineteenth-century context in which white represented purity and innocence, exemplified by the tradition of white wedding dresses at that time. In this context, readers may activate the schema WHITENESS IS INNOCENCE (Kha and Nhung, 2024: 43), meaning that Ahab's actions will be perceived as particularly evil.

In literature, the colour pink often characterises innocence. In *Lolita*, the pink attire worn by Lolita greatly contrasts with the sinister material of the novel. In this case the omnipresence of the colour pink contributes to dramatising the plot. For instance, the twelve-year-old Lolita is perceived as a sexual object *because* she wears pink; the colour is a symbol of youth, making Lolita a sexual object in the eyes of Humbert the paedophile (Plevíková, 2016: 74). The fact that Humbert is attracted to her bright, youthful clothing is metaphorically dark in itself. The colour pink works towards characterisation because the author seems to use their cultural schemas associating pink and innocence for their reader to experience the tension between innocence and duplicitousness in the text. *Lolita* offers a site of tension between schema reinforcement and schema disruption: the colour pink, according to a near-universal schema, represents youth and innocence (Koller, 2008: 396). Conversely, the very subject matter of the novel turns pink as the colour of sinfulness, thus potentially challenging the readers' schemas. Literature articulates the dialectic relationship between the universal and the individual. To understand a text, we typically activate our existing schemas (top-down approach). Yet, when reading the text, textual cues may activate, reinforce, refresh, or disrupt these existing schemas (bottom-up approach).

Finally, colours can be used to convey political ideologies such as parties (Burriss and McComb, 2001). For instance, in the American system, red typically represents the Republican party, whereas blue represents the Democrats. Communism is equally associated with the colour red. This also applies to political literature such as Stendhal's *Le Rouge Et Le Noir* (*The Red and the Black*) (1830/2020), which sees the evolution of the protagonist Julien, who aims to rise above his humble upbringing to reach higher social and political status. Pollard (1981) argues that since this bildungsroman was written during the French Restoration, red is likely to represent Jacobinism and black represents Clericalism; both colours are frequently referenced throughout the novel. Alternatively, red can be thought to reflect Napoleon's glory, whereas black symbolises the Restoration. The polarity of the two colours reflects Julien's political dilemma and the temptation he faces to betray his beliefs for an elevated social status. What this, and the other previous examples, suggest is that, in the context of colour in literature, schema activation relies on a pairing of a colour (something concrete) and an ideal or an ideology (something abstract). In this sense, colour symbolism – much like Conceptual Metaphor Theory (hereafter CMT) – relies on a stimulus–response pair, summarised by neuroscientists as 'neurons that fire together wire together' (see Section 3 for a more in-depth discussion on CMT). When a colour activates the same schema repeatedly, the schema becomes strengthened as a response.

This section highlights the entanglement between schemas and the use of colour concepts as symbols in literature. Since literary works are produced within a specific context with its specific meaning-making conventions, it would be surprising if literary works did not (re)produce some of the meanings already contained in the culture. After all, as Jean-Paul Sartre argues (1974: 275) that the writer cannot escape their 'insertion in the world, and [their] writing are the very type of a singular universal'. What stems from these observations is that the reading experience ultimately mobilises readers' schemas, relying on their existing mental reservoir of knowledge. The reading experience can either reinforce these schemas by representing them in a similar way or, perhaps less frequently, disrupt them by re-presenting them in a new way. In any case, colour symbolism relies, like CMT, on associative thinking: one concept becomes linked to another through iterative use.

2.4 Conclusion

In conclusion, this section has demonstrated that colour concepts cannot be reduced to simple descriptive terms; rather, they operate as complex linguistic and cultural resources. We showed that colours often function pragmatically, particularly when embedded in idiomatic expressions, where they convey affective and culturally specific meanings. This discussion highlighted how colour is deeply entangled with emotion, not only reflecting individual perception but also embodying shared cultural models. Building on this, the section illustrated how colour lexemes, by virtue of their descriptive precision and affective resonance, are particularly salient in literature, where they extend beyond scene-setting to act symbolically, index broader cultural schemas, and at times challenge entrenched associations. Taken together, the analyses underscore the cognitive linguistic perspective that colour meanings are constructed through conceptual mappings and schema activation, shaping both mental representations and interpretive practices. Thus, the section has traced a progression from the linguistic encoding of colour to its emotional and cultural resonances, and finally to its interpretive force in literature, showing how colour operates as a dynamic site of meaning-making at the intersection of language, culture, and cognition.

The decision to begin the Element with this cline, and to ground the analysis in examples from literature, is intentional. Literature provides a particularly rich site in which to observe both the perception and reception of colourful concepts, offering evidence of how colour terms are processed, interpreted, and extended beyond literal description. Starting with this range of examples establishes a foundation for the sections that follow, which approach colourful concepts from different but complementary angles. Section 3 considers colour in relation to metaphor and psychology, with a focus on pathetic fallacy as a point where natural description and emotional projection intersect. Section 4 shifts attention to the absence of colour, examining the lexeme colourless and its effects through a corpus-based study of Modernist literature. Taken together, these sections demonstrate the variety of contexts in which colourful concepts can be explored and the different kinds of impact they have, moving from lexical description to cultural resonance and literary interpretation.

3 Colour Concepts, Metaphor, and Psychology

This section builds on the schema analyses of Section 2 by examining how colour concepts operate metaphorically and psychologically, mapping emotions onto both vivid hues and muted tones. By analysing the metaphorical effects of colours on reader perception, Section 3 paves the way for Section 4's focus on the literary significance of *colourlessness*. In this section, we use pathetic fallacy, which links emotions to surroundings, as a case study. Our environment generally impacts our experiences because of the comfort (or lack thereof) it brings us (Grandjean et al., 1973; Persinger, 1975; Cunningham, 1979; Howarth and Hoffman, 1984; Baylis et al., 2018, amongst others). Colours are an inherent part of our surroundings and play 'an important role in our life. [...] Our experience with objects within our surroundings has a lot to do with our response to their colours. It is a visual language therefore it can give alert or warning, to reflect mood or to represent emotions' (Kumarasamy et al., 2014: 2). Pathetic fallacy (henceforth PF; a term coined by Ruskin (1856/2012)) is a literary technique that links surroundings and emotions, and as such PF can be used to underpin how emotions can be mapped onto surroundings. We use examples in literature taken from Pager-McClymont's corpus of PF (2021b) to evidence how this is achieved and link our findings to existing research in psychology, revealing that specific colours, colour descriptors, and tones are part of our conceptualisation of emotions.

3.1 Defining Pathetic Fallacy as a Metaphor

Pager-McClymont's recent works (2021a, 2021b, 2022, 2023) develop a model of PF which is formulated through an interdisciplinary lens. This was prompted by the necessity for a contemporary and methodical conceptual framework for PF, a concept featured in the English National Curriculum (Department for Education, 2013a, 2013b) and integrated into educational curricula. This model was constructed based on empirical data obtained from surveys administered to English educators. Notably, when asked to articulate their understanding of pathetic fallacy, 53% ($n = 134$) of respondents interpreted it as the projection of human emotions onto nature, while 36% construed it as a form of personification. The absence of a precise definition by the Department for Education and other educational materials produced by exam boards such as AQA or Edexcel leaves interpretation up to individual educators and education boards, thereby contributing to variations in how PF is conceptualised, leading to discrepancies surrounding its definition (for a more in-depth literature review, see Pager-McClymont (2021a)).

Pager-McClymont's construction of the PF model is underpinned by foregrounding theory (Miall and Kuiken, 1994; Van Peer, 2007; Leech,

2008), which elucidates how linguistic elements stand out within a text by means of parallelism, external deviation from linguistic norms, or internal deviation from established textual patterns. PF is defined by Pager-McClymont as *the projection of emotions onto surroundings by an animated entity, whether implicitly or explicitly depicted in the text*. This definition necessitates three criteria: the presence of an animated entity (implicit or explicit); vivid descriptions of the surroundings to facilitate readers' recognition of scene depictions and the mirroring effect of PF; and the depiction of emotions. Emotion encompasses various responses to internal or external events, with positive or negative valence, spanning mood, preferences, personality traits, and affective states, whether explicitly or implicitly conveyed in texts. Furthermore, three linguistic indicators akin to Short's (1996: 263) 'linguistic indicators of viewpoint' are identified for PF, encompassing imagery (figures of speech), repetition (lexis or syntax), and negation (lexical, morphological, and adverbial). Additionally, to date six effects of PF on narratives have been identified: foreshadowing; explicit communication of emotions; character development; building ambience; generating humour; and influence on readers' empathetic responses depending on specific mappings.

Pager-McClymont argues that PF is an extended metaphor (meaning that it can run on several paragraphs of text, as opposed to a single sentence or phrase, see Pager-McClymont, 2021b: 102) and can thus be analysed in terms of Conceptual Metaphor Theory (CMT). One of CMT's claims is that 'metaphor is primarily a matter of thought and action and only derivatively a matter of language' (Lakoff and Johnson, 1980: 153). This suggests that metaphors are part of our processing of the world around us before they are verbalised. CMT proposes that one conceptual domain A (the target domain) is understood in terms of another conceptual domain B (the source domain), and thus the metaphor is the cross-domain mapping (meaning correspondence) and can be phrased as such: A IS B (Lakoff and Johnson, 1980: 250; Kövecses, 2002: 5–6).

Metaphors that feature an emotion as a target domain (i.e., instances of PF) are labelled 'emotion metaphors' (Kövecses, 2008: 380). Kövecses explains that there is a link between conceptual metaphors and conceptual metonymies (a concept or object being referred to by substitution to one of its attributes (Wales, 2011: 267–268)). Indeed, certain physical manifestations of emotions or behaviours such as tears or turning away are 'conceptual metonymies' of emotions: they are single elements representing the emotion (Kövecses, 2008: 382). This is important to PF, as emotions can be present implicitly, thus requiring to be inferred. Conceptual metonymies of emotions allow readers to infer how a character might be feeling without the emotion needing to be explicitly expressed. For example, in the sentence 'she thought she missed him, and tears ran down her cheeks as she walked in the rain', the tears are metonymies of sadness, and the rain mirrors this sadness, as both the tears and the rain have the same downward motion.

Kövecses (2008: 382–383) also suggests that there could be a 'master metaphor' of emotions. According to his findings, primary emotions such as love or anger share a source domain: NATURAL FORCES. This is salient to PF, as the emotions expressed are the target domain and they are understood through the surroundings in the mirroring process. Consequently, the master metaphor of PF is EMOTION IS SURROUNDINGS (Pager-McClymont, 2022), and it can be linked to known conceptual metaphors such as Kövecses's EMOTION IS NATURAL FORCES (2008: 381) and Shinohara and Matsunaka's EMOTION IS EXTERNAL METEOROLOGICAL/ NATURAL PHENOMENON THAT SURROUNDS THE SELF (2009: 270). Others are linked to Lakoff and Johnson's 'orientational metaphor' (1980: 10–11) EMOTION IS VERTICAL ORIENTATION, as well as more creative metaphors such as EMOTION IS COLOUR TONE. This latter master metaphor is the focus of this section.

To analyse how the source domain (COLOURS) influences readers' perception of the target domain (EMOTIONS), we observe the saliency of the source domain. Stockwell (1999: 138) argues that saliency is 'more peculiar to the individual's worldview and culture, accumulated through social experience', thus the most salient aspect of the source domain might vary amongst individuals or texts. Stockwell (1999: 137) suggests that in the example of the 'image metaphor' given by Lakoff and Turner (1989: 90) 'my wife ... with the waist of an hourglass', the most salient characteristic perceived by readers is likely to be the shape of the hourglass as opposed to the cold glass it is made of or its sand. Therefore, in the analysis of PF as a conceptual metaphor, we discuss how the most salient characteristics of the source domains enable readers to mentally represent the emotions expressed (target domain). We also discuss how the cross-domain mapping between the emotion and the colour contributes to these effects of PF as identified in Pager-McClymont's model.

3.2 Emotions Are Colour Tones: Shades of Pathetic Fallacy

Our surroundings are significantly portrayed through colours (with the exception of individuals on the spectrum of (colour-)blindness). Colours are also used to express our emotions on a day-to-day basis: to 'feel blue', to 'see red', to be 'green with envy' (Jonauskaite et al., 2020b: 1). As discussed in Section 2.1, although these associations can vary from one culture or individual to another. Despite this, the association of colours and emotions can also occur naturally due to 'perceptual pairing': they are associations that arise directly from sensory experience (specifically, how the perception of a colour (e.g., seeing a red patch) triggers emotional or cognitive responses (based on Wang et al., 2014: 153; Jonauskaite et al., 2020b: 3)). Thus, emotional concepts are linked to abstract representations of colour concepts, rather than to specific perceptual or linguistic characteristics of colour, as we evidence later.

3.2.1 GOOD IS LIGHT AND BAD IS DARK

Metaphor researchers consensually discuss positive emotions in terms of 'light' and negative emotions in terms of 'dark', leading to the cross-domain mappings GOOD IS LIGHT (i.e., 'a bright day') and BAD IS DARK (i.e., 'dark thoughts') (Arnheim, 1969; Lakoff and Johnson, 1980: 50–53; Lakoff et al., 1991: 190; Meier and Robinson, 2005; Forceville and Renckens, 2013). According to Arnheim (1969: 313), these two associations 'go as far back as the history of man', and the affective link and contrast between light and darkness is due to the symbolic representation of good and evil. The texts included in this research feature multiple examples of colour tones as part of the surroundings that illustrate emotions. Most examples can be divided into two categories: light and dark. Therefore, the master metaphor that emerges is EMOTION IS COLOUR TONE, and since the colour tones are part of the surroundings, this mapping falls under the master metaphor of PF EMOTION IS SURROUNDINGS (see Pager McClymont, 2021b: 269–274).

Firstly, the mapping BAD IS DARK is prevalent. An example of this can be observed in Act II Scene II of *Macbeth* (Shakespeare, 1606/2014: 34–35):

> Lennox:
> The night has been unruly: where we lay,
> Our chimneys were blown down; and, as they say,
> Lamentings heard I' the air; strange screams of death,
> And prophesying with accents terrible
> Of dire combustion and confused events
> New hatch'd to the woeful time: the obscure bird
> Clamour'd the livelong night: some say, the earth
> Was feverous and did shake.

This scene is Lennox's description of the night King Duncan was murdered by Macbeth. The audience knows the murder occurred, but

Lennox does not. The three criteria of PF according to Pager-McClymont's definition are present: Lennox is the animated entity, and he expresses his anguish and worry over events of the nights through negative terms such as 'terrible', 'woeful' or 'lamentings'. This negative feeling is reflected by the dark surroundings (i.e., 'the night has been unruly' or 'obscure bird'). Lennox's BAD feeling of anguish is the target domain, and the DARK atmosphere of the scene is the source domain, thus providing the metaphor BAD IS DARK. In this instance, the opaque dark tone of the surroundings is the most salient characteristic of the source domain mapped onto the anguish expressed by Lennox (the target domain). This cross-domain mapping builds ambience (Stockwell, 2014: 365) and reinforces the suspense already present in the scene due to the dramatic irony or 'suspense paradox' (Carroll, 1996: 147–150) of Lennox not knowing of Duncan's murder whilst the audience is aware of it. Indeed, suspense relies on a level of uncertainty in a scene due to characters facing conflicting situations, and the tension of the suspense only lifts when a denouement occurs (Iwata, 2009: 253; see also Carroll, 1996). In the case of *Macbeth*, this occurs when the truth about King Duncan's murder is revealed.

Secondly, the mapping GOOD IS LIGHT is equally prevalent as BAD IS DARK. For instance, in chapter 11 of *Jane Eyre* (Brontë, 1847/2007), Jane describes her first morning at Thornhill:

> The chamber looked such a bright little place to me as the sun shone in between the gay blue chintz window curtains, showing papered walls and a carpeted floor, so unlike the bare planks and stained plaster of Lowood, that my spirits rose at the view. Externals have a great effect on the young: I thought that a fairer era of life was beginning for me, one that was to have its flowers and pleasures, as well as its thorns and toils.

The three criteria in Pager-McClymont's model of PF are present: Jane is the animated entity represented by the personal pronoun 'I'. Her feelings about Thornhill are explicitly positive ('gay', 'my spirit rose', 'fairer', 'pleasures'), as are the surroundings ('bright little place', 'sun shone', 'window'). In fact, the metaphor 'my spirit rose up' is in itself enclosed in the orientational metaphor GOOD IS UP (Lakoff and Johnson 1980: 10–11) to fully convey Jane's positive emotions. In addition to this metaphor, the use of PF projects Jane's feelings onto the 'bright' surroundings. In this instance Jane's positive emotions are the target domain and the light present in the scene through the sunshine and windows is the source domain, thus generating the cross-domain mapping GOOD IS LIGHT. The passage describes Jane's first impression of Thornhill, and this is particularly interesting, as so far in the narrative Jane has had mostly negative experiences in her life, such as living with the Reeds (her aunt and cousins) who tormented her, or struggling at Lowood charity school. However, she describes the room at Thornhill positively, thus creating a contrast with her past experiences. Indeed, a direct comparison is drawn by Jane herself between Thornhill and Lowood: '*unlike* the bare planks and stained plaster of Lowood' or 'fair*er* era of life was beginning for me' (our emphasis). This contrast in perception of surroundings foreshadows the rest of the plot, as eventually Jane and Mr Rochester will marry and live in Thornhill. Therefore, the use of PF with the mapping GOOD IS LIGHT signposts to readers how special Thornhill is in the development of the story.

The cross-domain mappings of BAD IS DARK and GOOD IS LIGHT are also present in *The Strange Case of Dr Jekyll and Mr Hyde* (Stevenson, 1886/2018), along with another colour metaphor: DISCOMFORT IS BROWN (see Pager-McClymont, 2021b: 271). The novel features a man with a split personality: Dr Jekyll, an academic, and Mr Hyde, his evil personality. As discussed, Arnheim (1969) suggests that the concept of light is associated with the concept of good, whereas the concept of dark is associated with evil. This aspect of the conceptual metaphors BAD IS DARK and GOOD IS LIGHT is salient to the characters of Jekyll and Hyde. Indeed, the first description of both characters occurs in chapter 2 (Stevenson, 1886/2018, our emphasis), in which Mr Utterson states: "this Master Hyde, if he were studied,' thought he, 'must have secrets of his own; *black* secrets, by the look of him; secrets compared to which poor Jekyll's worst would be like *sunshine*". The colour black (darkest colour tone possible) is associated with Hyde and the notion of light through 'sunshine' is associated with Jekyll, who is portrayed as a respectable and good character. Therefore, the conceptual metaphors BAD IS DARK and GOOD IS LIGHT are representative of the characters' personalities and the contrast between the two, thus contributing to their characterisation (see also Alter et al., 2016).

3.2.2 DISCOMFORT IS BROWN

In *The Strange Case of Dr Jekyll and Mr Hyde* (Stevenson, 1886/2018), GOOD IS LIGHT and BAD IS DARK are not the only conceptual mappings between colours and emotions. Indeed, as the story progresses and the boundaries between Hyde and Jekyll's personalities become blurred, the most prevalent colour present is brown, and it is often featured when other characters display emotions of anguish and discomfort. For instance, the passage further down is from chapter 10 and follows the Carew murder's discovery committed by Hyde (Stevenson, 1886/2018, our emphasis):

> A great *chocolate-coloured pall* lowered over heaven, but the wind was continually charging and routing these embattled vapours; so that as the cab crawled from street to street, Mr. Utterson beheld a marvellous number of degrees and *hues of twilight*; for here it would be dark like the back-end of evening; and there would be *a glow of a rich, lurid brown*, like the light of some strange *conflagration*; and here, for a moment, the fog would be quite broken up, and a haggard shaft of daylight would glance in between the swirling wreaths. The dismal quarter of Soho seen under these changing glimpses, with its *muddy* ways, and slatternly passengers, and its lamps, which had never been extinguished or had been kindled afresh to combat this *mournful reinvasion of darkness,* seemed, in the lawyer's eyes, like a district of some city in a nightmare.

The three criteria of PF are present, as Mr Utterson is the animated entity and the lexical field of death ('pall', 'wreath', and 'mournful') hints at Hyde committing murder. Mr Utterson displays negative feelings of anguish or discomfort ('embattled', 'lurid', 'strange', and 'nightmare'). The surroundings are mostly described through spatial deixis ('Soho', 'street to street', and 'cab') and through colour tones. Indeed, although the idea of 'darkness' is also present, brown is the colour used to describe the surroundings, not black: 'chocolate-coloured', 'hues of twilight', 'rich, lurid brown', and 'muddy'. Moreover, the term 'pall' not only reminds readers of Hyde's crime, but it also suggests decay that is typically of an earthy brown colour. Therefore, Mr Utterson's feeling of DISCOMFORT is the target domain mirrored by the source domain of the surroundings' BROWN tones, thus creating the cross-domain mapping DISCOMFORT IS BROWN. In this example, the brown tones of the surroundings build ambience but are also character-building. Indeed, brown is the colour obtained when all the other colours are mixed together: when light colours are mixed, light brown is obtained, when dark colours are mixed, dark brown or near-black colour is created (Edwards, 2004: 74). We argue that the prevalence of the colour brown in the passage following Hyde's crime is not coincidental: it implicitly conveys Jekyll and Hyde's mixed personalities.

Another example of DISCOMFORT IS BROWN is implicitly featured when the potion created by Dr Lanyon and Jekyll to dissociate himself from Hyde changes colours (Stevenson, 1886/2018, our emphasis):

> He sprang to it, and then paused, and laid his hand upon his heart; I could hear his teeth grate with the convulsive action of his jaws; and his face was so ghastly to see that *I grew alarmed both for his life and reason.*

> [...] I rose from my place with *something of an effort* and gave him what he asked.
>
> He thanked me with a smiling nod, measured out a few minims of the red tincture and added one of the powders. The mixture, which was at first of a *reddish hue*, began, in proportion as the crystals melted, to brighten in colour, to effervesce audibly, and to throw off small fumes of vapour. Suddenly and at the same moment, the ebullition ceased and the compound *changed to a dark purple,* which faded again more slowly to *a watery green.*

The colours of the potion are first red, then purple, and finally green ('first a reddish hue', 'changed to dark purple', 'watery green'). When those three colours are mixed, the colour obtained is brown (Edwards, 2004: 74). Dr Lanyon feels ill-at-ease with Jekyll's behaviour and the creation of the potion ('grew alarmed', 'something of an effort'). The colour brown – here the blend of all stages of the concoction – is a potential metonymy of the overall potion and its effect on the narrative. It is also the manifestation of Dr Lanyon's discomfort, suggesting he realises the impact the potion will have on Jekyll and Hyde's mixed personality. This example demonstrates that in literature, known conceptual metaphors such as GOOD IS LIGHT and BAD IS DARK are present but so are more novel instances of conceptual metaphors like DISCOMFORT IS BROWN. Each instance of metaphor associating emotions to colour concepts is an instance of PF and contributes to the process of building characters and ambience.

3.2.3 UNEASINESS IS GREY

Another example of a colour metaphor is UNEASINESS IS GREY, which can be observed in chapter 9 of *The Woman in Black* (Hill, 1983/2011):

> The first thing I noticed on the following morning was a change in the weather. As soon as I awoke, a little before seven, I felt that the air had a dampness in it and that it was rather colder and, when I looked out of the window, I could hardly see *the division between land and water, water and sky, all was a uniform grey, with thick cloud lying low over the marsh and a drizzle.* It was not a day calculated to raise the spirits and I felt unrefreshed and nervous after the previous night.

The passage takes place after Arthur and his dog Spider spend a night at Eel Marsh House, where supernatural and eerie events had previously occurred. PF's three criteria are present: Arthur is the first-person narrator ('I'), and he explicitly expresses his feelings of uneasiness ('I felt unrefreshed and nervous') after the events of the night, seemingly depressed to have awoken at the house and realising the events were not a dream.

The surroundings are described and the colour grey is dominant in this description (source domain), mirroring Arthur's negative emotions (target domain). The cross-domain mapping UNEASINESS IS GREY can thus be generated. The most salient characteristic of the colour grey mapped onto Arthur's feelings is the mix of black and white. Indeed, grey is a combination of those two tones, blurring them together, similarly to how the sea, the land, the sky, and the clouds are described in the previous extract. Additionally, the cloud and the drizzle, combined with the grey tones of the scene, could represent Arthur's uncertainty of the events of the previous night. Indeed, his judgement can be considered as clouded or foggy because he is unsure of what happened or of what he saw or heard.

Furthermore, the idea of uncertainty and uneasiness being emphasised through grey tones is also present in chapter 1 of *Dracula* (Stoker, 1897/2013):

> As we ascended through the Pass, the dark firs stood out here and there against the background of late-lying snow. Sometimes, as the road was cut through the pine woods that seemed in the darkness to be closing down upon us, great masses of greyness which here and there bestrewed the trees, produced a peculiarly weird and solemn effect, which carried on the thoughts and grim fancies engendered earlier in the evening, when the falling sunset threw into strange relief the ghost-like clouds which amongst the Carpathians seem to wind ceaselessly through the valleys.

The three criteria of PF in the model are present: the narrator describing the scene is Jonathan Harker and he is on a journey with Slovak men (hence the 'we' or 'us'). Harker's feelings of uneasiness and uncertainty are expressed through negative language (i.e., 'weird and solemn', 'grim', 'strange relief', and 'ghost-like'). The scene occurs at night and the surroundings are trees, mountains, and snow. Interestingly, the dominant colour of the surroundings is grey, as it is the only colour directly named ('greyness'). There is also a mix of two tones suggesting the overall dominance of the colour grey: the 'darkness' (here likely meaning black because of the night) is mixed with the 'ghost-like' clouds and the snow, both of which are white, thus emphasising the grey colour in the extract. Harker is not sure of where he is heading and the surroundings do not allow him to see what is around him, leading him to feel uncertain and uneasy (target domain) about his journey with the Slovaks. The grey colour of the surroundings (source domain) mirrors his uncertainty, thus generating the cross-domain mapping of PF UNEASINESS IS GREY. This correspondence has for effect to not only convey explicitly Harker's feelings but also to build the ambience of the scene and its suspense: Harker is uncertain of what will happen, and he is uncertain of what surrounds him; thus, one could say he is in a 'grey area' until he privy to the details of the journey. This last point is further developed in Section 3.4.

These analyses have demonstrated that PF as a conceptual metaphor maps the characters' emotions onto the surroundings (such as colours). Some of these metaphors are known conceptual metaphors (i.e., GOOD IS LIGHT, BAD IS DARK) and others are more novel, such as BROWN IS DISCOMFORT or UNEASINESS IS GREY. However, one can wonder if the association between those emotions and the specific colours of brown and grey also exists in the psychological impact of colours on human emotions. The next section aims to discuss this point and draws parallels between the correspondences observed in our analysis of literature and data from empirical studies in psychology.

3.3 Colour Surroundings and Psychology

So far in this section, the embraced position suggests that our perception of colours not only improves how we process events logically or through language but also influences our emotional responses by triggering positive or negative associations. (Sandford, 2011: 226–229). However, the emotional association with colours are 'not universal, nor are they applicable to any one entire population, since they are constructed with individual as well as collective participation' (Prado-León et al., 2006: 204; see also Prado-León et al., 2014). Certain studies claim that the psychological or emotional impact of colour on individuals lacks empirical support and that the topic is often misrepresented in popular culture (O'Connor, 2011: 234). Mohr et al. (2018: 230–233) suggest that some of the discussions surrounding the emotional impact of colour on individuals are inconclusive because 'affective connotations of colours are heterogeneous (for example, red represents anger and love) partly because they relate to different contexts' (Soriano and Valenzuela, 2009; Elliot and Maier, 2014; Dael et al., 2016; Sutton and Altarriba, 2016). Therefore, the way we perceive the connection between colour and emotion is dependent on context (i.e., positive or negative) and also on our own personal experiences such as culture or personality, especially when colours are used for symbolism (Baker 2004: 188; Elliot and Maier 2014). This shows that research on colour and emotion in psychology has faced significant methodological and conceptual critiques. Many studies rely on small or culturally specific samples, and affective responses to colour can vary widely depending on individual experience, context, and cultural background. In addition, popular accounts of colour–emotion associations often overstate the consistency or universality of these links, which are frequently more nuanced in empirical research. The studies discussed here are therefore not intended to establish universal psychological laws, but rather to provide illustrative evidence that patterns observed in literary portrayals of pathetic fallacy – where colour reflects or shapes emotional responses – are also reflected, to some extent, in empirical psychological research mapping emotions to surroundings. We thus draw on empirical research on specific colours to first examine whether the depiction of light and dark shades, as well as brown and grey in literature, is reflected in individuals' personal experiences. We then compare these observations with our findings from the previous literary analysis.

Empirical studies consensually corroborate the conceptual metaphors GOOD IS LIGHT and BAD IS DARK, as research shows that individuals tend to associate white/light tones with positive events or emotions, whereas black/dark tones are associated with negative events or emotions (Berlin and Kay, 1969; Edwards, 2004; Biggam and Kay, 2006; Biggam et al., 2011; Sandford, 2011). Additionally, Edwards (2004: 183–184) explains that brown is often seen as a dreary colour, despite its omnipresence in nature. It can symbolise misery or gloominess, for instance, 'to be in a brown study' means to be in deep thoughts. A study conducted by Prado-León et al. (2006) observes how Mexican participants emotionally perceive colours. Results reveal that grey is associated with emotions of sadness and fatigue, whereas brown is linked to dirtiness. Prado-León et al. (2006) compare their results to a study led by Mahnke (1996) that also looked at emotional reactions to colours but on Western cultured individuals. Prado-León et al. (2006: 210, our emphasis) make the following comparison:

> Mahnke found that only black and *grey were associated with mourning/ sorrow*, but, in our study, *brown was also associated with (6.2%) sadness*, even more so than black (5.1%). It is interesting that Mahnke reports that the same test was conducted in Europe in 1993 (Germany, Austria and Switzerland), and, in that study, *brown and violet appeared to be associated with sorrow/mourning.*

In *The Strange Case of Dr Jekyll and Mr Hyde*, the colour brown is associated with discomfort of other characters in the presence of Jekyll and Hyde's split personalities. However, the scene analysed provides a description of London after the Carew murder and the creation of the potion have taken place, allowing Hyde to take over Jekyll, freeing his inhibitions. In both scenes, the idea of 'dirtiness' can be found: London is described with the colour brown ('muddy') as it reflects the atmosphere of the city after the sin of murder was committed, thus suggesting the dirtiness of Hyde's soul now that he has committed the ultimate sin. Moreover, the colours of the potion when mixed create the colour brown, potentially suggesting that it will dirty Jekyll and Hyde's character by leading them to sins such as the Carew murder. Furthermore, both instances eventually lead to the idea of death, thus reflecting the results obtained by Prado-León et al. (2006) and Mahnke (1996), suggesting brown represents sadness or mourning.

Edwards (2004: 187–188) describes grey as 'the color of gloom and depression' and uses the song *Body and Soul* (1930) lyrics as an example: 'a future that's stormy, a winter that's gray and cold'. Grey also represents emotions of uncertainty or uneasiness. For instance, the phrase 'grey area' suggests an undetermined area or our uneasiness to label said area. In another study, Kumarasamy et al. (2014) analyse individuals' positive and negative reactions to specific colours. Although they did not observe any positive or negative trend for the colour brown (Kumarasamy et al., 2014: 9), the colour grey was seen mostly negatively, and they offer the following interpretation:

> Gray evoked the highest number of negative responses compared to black and was seen as the most negative because it is associated with rainy days and elicited sad or bored emotional responses. The emotions included sadness, depression, boredom, confusion, tiredness, loneliness, anger and fear. Reasons given for the negative emotional responses to gray shows that the colour gray tends to refer to bad weather, rainy, cloudy or foggy days and bring out the feelings of sadness, depression and boredom.

These observations are salient in our analysis of PF in *The Woman in Black* and *Dracula*. In *The Woman in Black* the narrator, Arthur, feels negative emotions such as uneasiness due to the supernatural events of the previous night, but he also feels sadness for yet again awakening at Eel Marsh House. These negative emotions are portrayed by the greyness of his surroundings, notably the bad weather ('thick clouds', 'drizzle'). In *Dracula*, the greyness of the surroundings is conveyed by the fog, but also the mix of the black of the trees in the night and the white of the snow, mirroring the narrator's uneasiness due to not knowing where he is going and his fear of the others on the same journey. These two literary examples reflect the findings observed in the empirical study conducted by Kumarasamy et al. (2014).

Overall, the literary analyses provided mirror the findings of the empirical psychological studies looking at correlations between emotions and colours. This means that the more novel cross-domain mappings of PF observed in the texts analysed in this research could in fact be more commonplace than originally thought, such as DISCOMFORT IS BROWN and GREY IS UNEASINESS. It also shows that the notion of 'surroundings' is a broad concept and can include anything from objects in a room (i.e., Jekyll and Hyde's potion) to natural elements in a scene (i.e., Eel Marsh in *The Woman in Black*), as argued by Pager-McClymont (2021b: 238). This section contributes to Pager-McClymont's view of surroundings in PF's mappings, as colours are an inherent part of our surroundings; thus, they can reflect emotions or even trigger them in certain instances (see Grandjean et al., 1973: 174; Persinger, 1975; Valdez and Mehrabian, 1994: 394; Yildirim et al. 2007: 3233; Saxbe and Repetti, 2010: 71–72). In the case of PF and its mapping EMOTIONS ARE COLOUR TONES, colours not only explicitly convey emotions and build the ambience of a scene (i.e., Lennox's anguish and suspense in *Macbeth*), but they are also character building (i.e., brown reflects Jekyll and Hyde's mixed personality) and they can foreshadow upcoming events such as the role Thornhill plays in Jane's story.

3.4 Conclusion

This section has demonstrated that colour is not only a descriptive feature of surroundings but also a central element in the metaphorical projection of emotions through PF. By examining examples across canonical texts, we observed how well-established mappings such as GOOD IS LIGHT and BAD IS DARK continue to structure literary representations of affect, while more novel mappings like DISCOMFORT IS BROWN and UNEASINESS IS GREY broaden our understanding of how emotions can be encoded. These mappings do more than mirror character states: they contribute to ambience, narrative tension, foreshadowing, and characterisation. As such, PF emerges as a particularly rich site for investigating how metaphor functions at the intersection of language, cognition, and aesthetics.

When considered alongside findings from psychology, these analyses underline the interdisciplinary value of studying colour–emotion correspondences. While research shows that such associations are not universal and vary across cultures and contexts, the parallels between literary portrayals and empirical data suggest that colour operates as a salient conceptual domain for encoding affective experience. By foregrounding colours as a key aspect of surroundings within PF, this section extends

Pager-McClymont's model and highlights how colour metaphors provide insight into both literary technique and human psychology. Ultimately, this convergence invites further exploration into how readers process the interaction between environment and emotion, and how literature both reflects and shapes our perceptual and emotional lives.

4 Absence of Colour Concepts: *Colourlessness* in Literary Prose

This section builds on the analyses of Sections 2 and 3 by turning to the absence of colour, using a mixed-methods approach that incorporates corpus analysis to examine how colourlessness functions in literary prose and how it becomes a powerful interpretative resource. Indeed, in this section we present a broad survey of the lexeme *colourless* in nineteenth- and twentieth-century prose. This research is corpus-based, whilst cognitive linguistic tools such as metaphor and schemas are used to interpret the findings and showcase their impact on readerly experience. The use of a corpus allows us to identify characteristics and patterns of language to provide a replicable and reliable literary critical position on how the term is employed in a sample of prose representative of an entire literary movement: Modernism. Throughout the section, we use the following definitions: the literal meaning of the term *colourless* is 'having no colour; transparent, clear' ('colourless', 2024). The OED defines a *colour* as 'any of the constituents into which light can be separated as in a spectrum or rainbow; any particular mixture of these constituents; a particular hue or tint' ('colour', 2024).

4.1 Research Corpora and Methodology

The methodology was selected to establish a relationship between the notions put forth by the concept of colourlessness and the literary employment of the term. Corpus-based research can aid in the systematic identification of language patterns and linguistic deviations, consolidating intuited impressions. Insights can be delivered into recurring features of literary style by providing empirical evidence that identifies and confirms salient conclusions (Simpson, 2014). As summarised by Mahlberg and McIntyre:

> A major benefit of using corpus techniques to aid stylistic analysis is that this practice enables us to address what has long been an issue with the analysis of prose fiction. This is the problem of length and the fact that most prose texts are simply too long for the stylisticians to deal with. (Mahlberg and McIntyre, 2011: 205)

The application of corpus stylistics research methodologies does not replace literary or textual analysis, but instead works in conjunction to identify and quantify linguistic features, enabling generalisations to be made about the language within a text. The data analysis approaches chosen to examine the research findings are firmly grounded in established linguistic and stylistic frameworks, allowing for an in-depth understanding of the lexeme *colourless* in Modernist prose and cognitive linguistic tools are employed to interpret patterns.

4.1.1 Corpora Selection

Focusing on a single word requires a large number of texts to allow salient conclusions to be drawn, resulting in the need for digital editions due to the vast amount of text being searched and analysed. Additionally, complete passages were needed to develop a clear understanding of the context, meaning, and usage of *colourless*. These criteria negated the use of popular corpora such as the British National Corpus and the Corpus of Contemporary American, as the co-text required for a thorough analysis is often not readily available. Initially, three corpora containing nineteenth- and twentieth- century prose texts were selected for study: CLiC 19th Century Reference (Mahlberg et al., 2020);[2] CLiC Dicken's Novels (Mahlberg et al., 2020); and HUM19UK.[3]

The CLiC corpora website allows for simple searches on one or more terms for each of the corpora available within the online application. The HUM19UK corpus is comprised of 100 complete British novels published between the years 1800 and 1899. There is no search facility available for HUM19UK, so the texts were downloaded and examined using the search capabilities of Windows Explorer. A total of forty-six texts in all three corpora contained the lexeme *colourless*.

The lexeme *colourless* occurs fifteen times in the CLiC Dickens corpus and there are twenty-six instances in the CLiC 19th Century corpus. Additionally, the word *colorless* with the American spelling is found nine times in the CLiC 19th Century corpus, resulting in thirty-five uses of the lexeme in the two corpora. There are fifty-eight occurrences in total of *colourless* in the HUM19 corpus. The text with the highest frequency is *Shirley* (1849) by Charlotte Brontë, containing the lexeme *colourless* seven

---

[2] Available at: https://clic.bham.ac.uk/
[3] Available at: www.uu.se/en/department/english/research/english-linguistics/electronic-resource-projects/hum19uk-huddersfield-utrecht-uppsala-middelburg-corpus-of-19th-century-british-fiction

times. Two texts in the HUM19 corpus both have six occurrences of colorless: *Under Two Flags* (1867) by Louise de la Ramee and *Robert Elsmere* (1888) by Mary Augusta Ward. As there were only fifty-eight passages and three texts written by three authors, we concluded that the HUM19 corpus would also not provide a diverse representation of the notions put forth by *colourless* in prose. As these three corpora are comprised of nineteenth-century prose, we made the decision to create a bespoke corpus of Modernist prose (see Section 4.1.2), speculating there would be a large number of texts available in digital format, offering significantly more examples of *colourless* to examine and research. Our findings show that 144 texts use the lexeme colourless in the bespoke corpus – at least four times more than the corpora discussed earlier. The following sub-section explains how the corpus was created and the selection criteria used to identify those texts warranting further analysis.

4.1.2 The Modernist Literature Project

Modernism as a literary movement is characterised by the rise of industrialisation and development of the modern world in Europe and the United States between the end of the nineteenth century and the beginning of the twentieth century and was particularly shaped by World War I. In both poetry and prose fiction, modernism is defined by an intentional departure from conventional literary methods (Childs, 2008; Parsons, 2014).

We use the *Modernist Literature Project*[4] (henceforth MLP; McClure and Pager-McClymont, 2022) as the starting point for this study. Presently, the MLP contains over 20 million words, 328 texts, and 31 authors. The corpus offers Modernist prose fiction, shorter prose, and poetry as well as sub-corpora for specific authors and themes. Each text has been processed by Wmatrix[5] (Rayson, 2009) to create parts-of-speech and semantic domain tagsets that are also available on the website. The MLP includes only digital versions of texts that exist in the public domain to avoid copyright issues as the corpus is freely accessible. Therefore, some works from canonical Modernist authors such as Joyce and Hemmingway are not included.

4.1.3 Methodology

We chose a corpus-based approach grounded in stylistic frameworks to aid in the identification of the lexeme *colourless* in Modernist prose, thus

---

[4] Available at: https://modernistliteratureproject.org/. This project was funded by the Poetics and Linguistics Association (PALA).
[5] Available at: http://ucrel.lancs.ac.uk/wmatrix/

avoiding an oversimplified process of general passage selection. After we retrieve potential occurrences of the term, close reading and qualitative analysis are necessary. As noted by Mahlberg (2009), a main benefit of corpus stylistics is methodological eclecticism, adding systematicity to literary analysis. Provided in the following sections is a detailed discussion of how the texts were selected and the data analysis frameworks that are applied in our research, addressing the concepts put forth by the lexeme *colourless* in Modernist works. Following Mahlberg and Smith (2010), quoted extracts that are presented in this section will not have page numbers, as these often do not exist for the electronic versions of texts.

4.1.4 Selection of Modernist Texts Employing Colourless

We examined the MLP corpus using the search capabilities of Windows Explorer. Twenty authors in the corpus employ the term *colourless* in their prose, resulting in 144 texts containing the lexeme. As the focus of this research is on a single lexeme, we did not feel unequal balance in total texts amongst Modernist authors would negatively affect the reliability of our results; the aim of our analysis is to show how *colourless* is employed in Modernist prose and our research findings are not purely reliant on quantitative analysis. The authors and corresponding frequency counts are shown in Table 1.

Texts from the first four authors comprise over 50% of the results. In the nine texts authored by Kipling that contain *colourless*, there are eleven occurrences of the term. Although Richardson only has seven texts, there are twenty-one individual occurrences of the lexeme. We concluded that our research corpus would focus on authors that employed the term twenty or more times. The resulting frequency counts of *colourless* for these four authors are shown in Table 2.

To summarise, the research corpus is comprised of eighty-five texts which contain the lexeme *colourless* that are written by these four authors.

Once we determined the 4 authors under study that employed *colourless* more than 20 times, approximately 400 to 500 words of co-text for each occurrence were selected, resulting in 164 passages. However, Conrad, Richardson, and Wharton employ the lexeme twice within a single co-text selection. Wharton also uses *colourless* twice within a single co-text selection in *The Children* (1928), and *colorless* twice intrasententially in the text *In Morocco* (1920). In *The Tunnel* (1919), Richardson employs the adverbial form *colourlessly* in a reporting clause and then 148 words further in the text uses the word *colourless*. Taking into consideration these

Table 1 Modernist corpus texts containing *colourless*

Author	Texts
James	35
Wharton	23
Conrad	20
Kipling	9
Richardson	7
Lawrence	6
Maugham	6
Woolf	6
Wilde	6
Anderson	4
Fitzgerald	4
Madox Ford	3
Orwell	3
Mann	2
Joyce	2
Pound	2
Huxley	2
Dos Passos	2
Eliot	1
Lewis	1

Table 2 Frequency of *colourless* in selected authors.

Author	Texts	Freq
James	35	57
Conrad	20	46
Wharton	23	45
Richardson	7	21

5 incidences of the lexeme occurring twice within a co-text extract results in a total of 169 occurrences contained within 164 extracts in the 85 texts being studied.

4.1.5 Conducting Stylistic Analyses: Foregrounding and Conceptual Metaphor Theories

The employment of 400 to 500 words of co-text allows us to compare how the passage fits within the wider context of the text itself. To systematically analyse the extracts, we use two stylistic theories. The first is the theory of foregrounding (Mukařovský, 1932/1964; Miall and Kuiken, 1994; Kuiken et al., 2004; Leech and Short, 2007; Leech, 2008), which underpins how specific elements of language stand out against the rest of the text. This foregrounding can occur:

- by internal deviation, meaning the text deviates from its own established pattern (i.e., a non-rhyming stanza in a poem that otherwise only features rhymes);
- by external deviation, the text deviates against the norm of the language (here, English), such as idiomatic expressions;
- by parallelism, such as repeated terms or structures.

We specifically focus on foregrounded elements, showing how the authors use the lexeme *colourless* in their prose.

As shown in Section 4.1.4 we observe that the term was frequently used metaphorically. Thus, we draw on CMT (see Section 3.1) to analyse the extracts where one concept is understood in terms of another. However, in certain metaphorical expressions, one of the domains is alluded to by one of its components: these are conceptual metonymies of those domains. Metonymies are tropes in which concepts are referred to or substituted by one of their attributes (Wales, 2011). Kövecses argues that it is possible for the physical manifestation of emotions to allude to the emotion metaphor cross-domain mapping. Kövecses (2008: 382) states:

> the metonymies can be said to motivate the metaphors. This motivation is not simply linguistic or conceptual but also physical, in the sense that the metonymies indicate certain physical aspects of the body involved in emotion. The physical aspect indicated by emotion metonymies can be factored into two types: behavioral and physiological.

For example, in the sentence *she smiled when she saw him*, the smile is a conceptual metonymy of happiness. This aspect of metaphor mapping is particularly salient to our analysis of *colourless*, and it contributes to the mapping ANATOMY IS MIND in our corpus, as discussed in Section 4.2.2.

4.1.6 A Note on Orthography

As it is important to allow for the replication of our methodological approaches, we discuss the challenge presented by the Australian and British spelling of *colourless* in contrast to the American *colorless*. Numerous Modernist authors, including James, Kipling, Richardson, and Wharton, use both conventions in their works but show a preference for one spelling over the other. We were concerned that this may be a general problem with the country-specific transcription of digital texts. Therefore, we examined printed copies of two randomly selected texts by a British and American author – *Aaron's Rod* and *In Morocco* – and the spelling in the printed version is the same as the digital editions.

4.2 Findings

To present our findings, we first review the four Modernist authors that employ the lexeme *colourless* most often, as well as how they each use *colourless* as a stylistic device. We then discuss the metaphorical implication of *colourless* and the opposition it creates. Lastly, patterns observed in the extracts through the prevalence of negation and lexical parallelisms are presented.

4.2.1 The Use of Colourless by Four Modernist Authors

As discussed in Section 4.1.4, four authors in our Modernists corpus employed the term *colourless* more than twenty times:

- James employs *colourless* fifty-seven times across thirty-five texts;
- Conrad employs it forty-six times across twenty texts;
- Wharton employs it forty-five times across twenty-three texts;
- Richardson employs it twenty-one times across seven texts.

As stated, there are 169 occurrences of *colourless* in 85 prose works written by the 4 authors under study. In the following sections, we first present each of the authors' use of the term, listed in ascending order of number of occurrences. We then provide a foregrounding analysis, progressing to a discussion of similarities and differences between the writers. Tables 3–6 list multiple functions for a single occurrence of *colourless*. Thus, the total number might not correspond to the figures in Table 3. For example, in the reporting clause 'he said colourlessly', the adverb *colourlessly* contributes to characterisation in addition to the representation of events.

Our first author of interest is James, who is often considered one of the most well-known Modernists. His style is often described as intricate because of the complex syntax and juxtaposition used in his writing (Watanabe, 1962; Simon, 2007). The effect on readers is to leave them feeling 'uneasy and disoriented as some of his characters are' because his style creates ambiguity to climax potential dénouements (Cross and Berger, 1993: 1). Table 3 summarises how James uses the lexeme *colourless* in his prose.

Table 3 Henry James's uses of *colourless*

Use of term *colourless* or *colorless*	Number of times *colourless* occurs across 29 novels
To refer to behaviour or to personality trait	15
For physical description	13
To refer to surroundings	7
To refer to events or actions	9
To describe tone of voice	9
Used literally to mean 'transparent'	4
Used by women	22
Used by men	24
Used by omniscient narrator	11

James uses *colourless* to describe the characters' personality traits through their physical appearance and to hint at their negative traits since the term is systematically used negatively. James employs *colourless* to indicate pale or white, but his use is divergent from the other three authors as he does not consistently add additional colour term pairings. However, when the term is used with other colours such as 'olive', as evidenced in Section 4.2.2 example (1) further, then *colourless* becomes oxymoronic, which can be considered to contribute to his complex style of combining contradictory extremes.

Our second author of interest is Conrad, who drew on his personal experiences, namely of being a sailor, to inform his plots and characters. He embraces modernism in his capacity to provide psychological depth through layers of narration while showing the moral ambiguity of his characters. Conrad's narration subtly deals with the reality of the good and bad of the world with scepticism (Graham, 1996). His use of third-person narration allows for narrative perspective and distance, potentially allowing him to maintain focus on his characters and sombre tales (Lothe, 1996). Table 4 summarises the different uses of *colourless* employed by Conrad.

In contrast to James, Conrad uses *colourless* in the negative portrayal of surroundings and anatomy, particularly in descriptions of lips, face, and tone of voice. *In The Secret Agent*, Conrad presents the bomb-throwing character as the Lombrosean type of the 'born criminal' through negative facial features. Conrad employs the term *colourless* six times to indicate the colour black or darkness and there are twelve occurrences that mean pale or white. As such, the oxymoronic aspect of the term is emphasised and strengthened. In Conrad's forty-six texts, *colourless*

Table 4 Conrad's uses of *colourless*

Use of term *colourless* or *colorless*	Number of times *colourless* occurs across 29 novels
To refer to behaviour or to personality trait	5
For physical description	21
To refer to surroundings	17
Used literally to mean 'transparent'	2
To refer to characters' 'words'	1
To refer to objects	2
Used by women	10
Used by men	16
Used by omniscient narrator	21

is paired with *black* twenty-nine times and *white* twenty-five times, further reinforcing the oxymoronic use and contrasting the definition of the term. Conrad's use of *colourless* corroborates elements of his style so far discussed, highlighting his scepticism when describing characters and their surroundings.

Our third author of interest is Wharton, who embodies values of Modernism by drawing on her womanly experiences of breaking from the Victorian Era and the effects of World War I. Her narratives often portray the mundane and brutal aspect of life for women during this time of upheaval (Haytock, 2008). Although she did not consider herself a Modernist, the scepticism and the 'uneasy dialogue' portrayed in her writing arguably show commonalities with other Modernists (Herman, 2001; Ware, 2004). Wharton also has varied uses of the term *colourless*, as evidenced in Table 5.

Wharton is the only one of our four authors to use *colourless* twice as often in the description of female characters as for male characters. Wharton often employs the term to describe the physical characteristics of female characters or the affairs of their everyday life. In contrast to male characters, where there is no mention of the term in this context, the lexeme *colourless* often stresses the negative aspect of female habits and existence, mirroring her unique feminine Modernist view of the world expressed through her engagement with gender issues and broader feminist discourse (Ammons, 1980). The lexeme is also associated with the notion of vagueness through the lexical field of unknown, including the terms *smoke*, *blurred*, *mists*, *grey*, and *shadow*. This concept could be linked to the metaphorical mapping of UNCERTAINTY IS GREY (see Section 3.2.3).

Table 5 Edith Wharton's uses of *colourless*

Use of term *colourless* or *colorless*	Number of times *colourless* occurs across 29 novels
To refer to behaviour or to personality trait	6
For physical description	15
To refer to surroundings	3
To refer to characters' lives, habits, and long-term emotions	21
Used literally to mean 'transparent'	1
Used to describe the English language	1
Used by women	29
Used by men	12
Used by omniscient narrator	4

Table 6 Richardson's uses of *colourless*

Use of term *colourless* or *colorless*	Number of times *colourless* occurs across 29 novels
To refer to tone of voice	6
For physical description	5
To refer to surroundings	7
Used literally to mean 'transparent'	1
To describe actions or characters' behaviour	1
Used by women	9
Used by men	3
Used by omniscient narrator	8

Similarly to Wharton, Richardson draws on her own womanly experiences and the tragedies of her life such as her mother's suicide to inspire her writing. Her fiction 'transgress[es] boundaries' despite their shorter nature and show a 'strong resistance to obvious or fixed meanings and are mostly uncertainly ended, opening out, inviting speculation and interpretation' (Drewery, 2016: 4). The complexity of her style stems from her 'fragmented syntax' allowing for stream of consciousness, the use of varied narrative viewpoints, and 'unconventional plot developments' (Frost, 2002: 273). The language of Modernist prose adopted this style to 'transcribe thought, perception, and emotion at the moment before it is fully articulated in the mind' (Sotirova, 2013: 40). Table 6 illustrates how

Richardson employs the lexeme *colourless* in the prose contained in the Modernist corpus:

Like Conrad, Richardson uses *colourless* to represent the oppositional concepts created by the terms pale or white and black or darkness. The lexeme *colourless* is associated with the term black fourteen times and twenty times to white, further emphasising the contrast. There are twenty occurrences of the colour grey in the immediate co-text of *colourless*, reinforcing Richardson's use of it to represent black or darkness and pale or white, as grey is the blend of these colour tones. As we found with Wharton, Richardson mostly employs *colourless* in reference to female characters or an omniscient narrator. This is frequently accomplished through descriptions of scene surroundings and character anatomy such as face, lips, and voice. For instance:

(1) 'I caught a glimpse of an unprepossessing countenance – despite rather good features and fine hair – the most striking characteristics of which were a missing front tooth and lips that hung loose and colorless', *The Long Day* (Richardson, 1905).
(2) 'Surprised into amazement, Miriam looked up to consult the face of Jessie Wheeler, the last speaker – a tall flat-figured girl with a strong squarish pale face, hollow cheeks, and firm colourless lips', *Backwater* (Richardson, 1916).
(3) 'Her will and the shapeless colourless voice murmuring from the back of her throat were given to the lesson', *Interim* (Richardson, 1919).
(4) 'In the colourless moaning voice with which she agreed that there was much for her to see in London and that she had many things she wished particularly not to miss', *Revolving Lights* (Richardson, 1923).

Strikingly, when Richardson uses the term, it is within a negative context, highlighting the scepticism likely generated by her own traumas of financial hardship, parental suicide, and the miscarriage of her out-of-wedlock child with H. G. Wells (DorothyRichardson.org, 2025).

The quantitative and qualitative analyses of the lexeme colourless as employed by the four authors under study highlighted commonalities and differences in their stylistic use of the term. The similarities are of particular interest, and we thus analyse them in greater detail in the following three sections. To summarise, there are five distinct and frequent occurrences of *colourless* being used as a stylistic device and these are presented in Table 7. Although other researchers may categorise these incidents differently, ours is informed by the focus of this research on foregrounding analysis.

Table 7 Comparison of uses of *colourless* between James, Conrad, Wharton, and Richardson

Use of term *colourless* or *colorless*	Freq in 169 occurrences	%
Physical description in allusion to personality traits	53	32
Description of surroundings	33	20
To describe life events, actions, or behaviour	30	18
In reference to personality	25	15
Used literally to mean transparent	8	5

The lexeme *colourless* is used 32% of the time to describe physical descriptions of characters, often alluding to their personality traits. It is the only usage of the term that is employed similarly across all four authors; thus, a further discussion is presented in Section 4.2. The other uses of *colourless* reflect the authors' idiosyncrasies. However, the use of morphological negation in the lexeme *colour<u>less</u>* (see Section 4.3) to describe events, surroundings, or characters' personalities is typical of Modernism. This mirrors each of the authors' style as reviewed, representing the changes of the world with scepticism and embracing the harshness of reality. Our analyses reflect this despite its focus being on the use of *colourless* in physical descriptions.

4.2.2 The Lexeme Colourless as Conceptual Metonymy, Oxymoron, and Opposition

The lexeme *colourless* is used by James, Conrad, Wharton, and Richardson in a stylistically similar metaphorical manner. As established in Section 4.1, the term *colourless* literally means having no colour – being transparent or clear. In contrast, the term *colour* refers to any component of light seen in a spectrum or rainbow, or any specific hue or tint. Black and white are also defined as colours, black being 'the darkest colour possible' whereas white is 'the lightest colour possible' ('black', 2024; 'white', 2024). However, it is recorded in Table 7 that the literal sense of *colourless* is only employed 5% of the time by the four authors. This allows us to conclude that 95% of the occurrences in the Modernist corpus of the lexeme *colourless* are employed as a figurative stylistic device. The OED's (2024) figurative definition for *colourless* is 'having no distinctive character, vividness, or intensity; lacking in interest; bland'. Our analysis is carried out using CMT, allowing for salient conclusions to be drawn on how the authors' usage of *colourless* is figurative and the ensuing impact this has on readers' mental representation of *colourless* descriptions. We argue that this phenomenon stems from *colourless* being an inherent lexeme of imagery.

Even though several definitions of *imagery* exist, scholars agree that it incorporates the auditory, visual, kinaesthetic, olfactive, and tactile senses (Halpern, 1988; Finke, 1989; Nanay, 2015, 2017, 2018; Anderson, 2021). Dancygier (2014: 214) investigates the notion of imagery in relation to readers' perspective, focusing on bodily experiences linked to the senses. They state:

> mental imagery can be used figuratively, to evoke other meanings (as in metaphor, simile, allegory, etc.). This pathway to meaning construction is in fact quite common, as the study of conceptual metaphor suggests. It seems to rely on a somewhat different pattern of evocation. Every image evokes frames of some kind, but it can evoke more than one, often based on the perceived links across different areas of experience.

Dancygier (2014) employs Abrams and Harpham's idea that imagery generates in readers' minds 'vivid and particularized' mental images, commenting on the rich yet subjective experience this entails (2005: 128). Pager-McClymont (2021a: 125) defines imagery as the text's formation of a vivid image using sensory language that elicits a mental image in the mind of readers. Figurative language and metaphors function as imagery when they engage the senses, prompting readers to form mental images based on their own physical and sensory experiences: since readers usually share those senses, they can relate to the descriptions and visualise the scene through personal experiences and memory (Boerger, 2005; see also Nanay, 2015, 2018). Green (2017) distinguishes between 'image-permitting' metaphors which allow for mental representation of images, and 'image-demanding' metaphors which necessitate the creation of a mental image to properly comprehend the metaphor. This is salient to our analysis of *colourless* as an oxymoron and as a factor in the conceptual metaphor ANATOMY IS MIND because the lexeme is an inherent form of imagery, as it draws on visual senses. In this metaphor, characters' physical traits (pale faces, wan expressions, or colourless voices) are not merely literal descriptions of appearance but serve as a window into their psychological or emotional states. The abstract domain of 'mind' or 'personality' is understood via the concrete domain of 'body', so that anatomical features function as a proxy for mental and emotional life.

The first figurative usage of *colourless* is the association with other colours in the immediate co-text of the extracts, and this is observed for all four authors as shown:

(1) 'After I had left the town I became more intimate with that Provencal charm which I had already enjoyed from the window of the train, and which *glowed* in the sweet sunshine and the *white* rocks, and lurked in the smoke-puffs of the little *olives*. The *olive*-trees in Provence are half the landscape. They are neither so tall, so stout, nor so richly contorted as I have seen them beyond the Alps; but this mild <u>colorless</u> bloom seems the very texture of the country', *A Little Tour In France* (James, 1884).

(2) 'Linda pouted, advancing her *red* lips, which were almost too *red*; but she had admirable eyes, *brown*, with a sparkle of *gold* in the irises, full of intelligence and meaning, and so clear that they seemed to throw a glow upon her thin, <u>colourless</u> face', *Nostromo: A Tale of the Seaboard* (Conrad, 1904).

(3) 'That the moment one wanted to hold fast to was not, in most lives, the moment of keenest personal happiness, but the other kind – the kind that would have seemed *grey* and <u>colourless</u> at first, the moment when the meaning of life began to come out from the mists', *The Fruit of the Tree* (Wharton, 1907).

(4) 'There were shabby drawing room chairs standing in an irregular row on the dirty *grey* stone, railed by a balustrade of *dark maroon* painted iron railings almost <u>colourless</u> with *black* grime. But the elastic outer air was there and away at the end of the street a great *gold pink* glow stood above and showed through the feathery upper branches of the trees in Endsleigh Gardens', *Interim* (Richardson, 1919).

As the examples show, other colours are used in the same descriptions that feature *colourless*, such as red, gold, brown, white, pink, and grey. Therefore, in the immediate co-texts, the use of *colourless* is oxymoronic: two opposite concepts are juxtaposed to one another. The association of contrasting concepts generates a rich and complex mental representation for readers. This joins Chomsky's idea (1956: 116) that the 'colorless green ideas sleep furiously' is, although grammatically correct, nevertheless semantically nonsensical. Part of the meaning is deprived because of the association of *colorless* with the colour green, creating an oxymoron. Additionally, as we discussed in Section 3.1, Conrad and Richardson both employ *colourless* to mean black or darkness and white or light. Further illustrated in example (2) earlier is the phenomenon with 'colourless face' implying a face that is so pale it is almost deprived of colour. Whereas, *colourless* in example (4) is directly associated with iron railings that are almost black. Therefore, it could be argued that in these contexts the lexeme *colourless* is its own opposite.

The second figurative use of *colourless* occurs in descriptions of characters' physical appearance. In a wider co-text, the term most often refers to the characters' personality traits. For instance:

(5) 'I have had this opportunity more than once, for I have met him at Tours, at Nantes, at Bourges; and everywhere he is suggestive. But he has the defect that he is never pictorial, that he never by any chance makes an image, and that his style is perversely <u>colorless</u>, for a man so fond of contemplation. His taste is often singularly false; it is the taste of the early years of the present century', *A Little Tour in France* (James, 1884).

(6) 'The emotion, however, was but meagrely expressed in the flatness with which she heard herself presently say: 'I'll go to the Registrar now'. 'Now?' Magnificent was the sound Mrs Gereth threw into this monosyllable. 'And pray who's to take you?' Fleda gave a <u>colorless</u> *smile*, and her companion continued: 'Do you literally mean that you can't put your hand upon him?' Fleda's wan *grimace* appeared to irritate her; she made a short, imperious *gesture*', *The Spoils of Poynton* (James, 1896).

(7) 'This feeling accounts for nine tenths of their *audacious gestures*. Her face had gone completely <u>colourless</u>. *Ghastly*. Fancy having it brought home to her so *brutally* that she was the sort of person who must run away from the police! I believe she was *pale with indignation*, mostly, though there was, of course, also *the concern for her intact personality, a vague dread of some sort of rudeness*', *A Set of Six* (Conrad, 1908).

(8) 'Their own faces were *sallow* with the unwholesomeness of hot air and sedentary toil, rather than with any actual signs of want: they were employed in a fashionable millinery establishment, and were fairly well clothed and well paid; but the youngest among them was as *dull* and <u>colourless</u> as the middle-aged', *House of Mirth* (Wharton, 1905).

(9) 'At the end of an hour spent pacing the half-dark platform exhausted with cold and excitement and the monotonously reiterated effort to imagine the arrival of one of Mrs. Hungerford's heroines from a train journey, Miriam, whose costume had been described in a letter to the girl's mother, was startled wandering amidst the vociferous passengers at the luggage end of the newly arrived train by a *liquid* <u>colourless</u> *intimate voice* at her elbow', *Backwater* (Richardson, 1916).

(10) 'Sissie read her set of phrases in heavy *docility*. Her will and the *shapeless <u>colourless</u> voice murmuring* from the *back of her throat* were given to the lesson; but the kindly sullen profile smouldered in slumber', *Interim* (Richardson, 1919).

These six passages help to illustrate that physical descriptions of faces, mannerisms, bodily actions, and expressions can be used to convey characters' personality traits. As such, the anatomical description becomes a conceptual metonymy for the characters' mind, allowing for the cross-domain mapping of ANATOMY IS MIND (Kövecses, 2008: 382). The characters' mind, an abstract target domain, is understood through their anatomical description, which is a concrete source domain.

Overall, *colourless* is used as a factor in the conceptual metaphor ANATOMY IS MIND and as an oxymoron, which are a type of imagery triggering a visual sensory response. As such, when *colourless* is used figuratively, it is an image-permitting metaphor (Green, 2017). This allows readers to have a rich and comprehensive mental representation of the characters, as their personalities are represented and embodied by their physical or visual appearances. Indeed, by mapping mental states onto bodily traits, readers are prompted to infer characters' emotions and dispositions from visible features, engaging in an embodied form of comprehension that enriches their mental representation of the narrative.

4.2.3 Negative Co-Text of Term Colourless

Another finding from our foregrounding analysis of the lexeme *colourless* is the prevalence of negation in the extracts' co-text. Negation is a way to build propositions: for each P proposition that is true, there is a ~P proposition that exists that is false (Hidalgo-Downing 2000a, 2000b; Giovanelli 2013). It is argued by Leech (1983) that positive propositions are more informative than negated ones, and thus choosing to negate a proposition foregrounds the information conveyed by the negation, noting there are exceptions. For instance, the sentence *She is not a teacher* is not as informative as *She is a doctor*. However, stating *My cat is not female* is equally informative as *My cat is male*.

There are different types of stylistic and linguistic negation and three are prominent in our study. Firstly, syntactic negation involves the adverbs 'not' or 'never' (e.g., she is *not* a teacher), and is thus marked (Tottie, 1991; Hidalgo-Downing, 2003; Nørgaard, 2007). Secondly, morphological or affixal negation is also marked and involves the use of prefixes or suffixes to negate a term (e.g., colour*less*, *un*happy). Thirdly, lexical or inherent negation is unmarked, but 'it corresponds to the value which tends to be assigned to a term in opposition to a "positive" term (good/bad, dead/alive, crazy/sane)' (Hidalgo-Downing, 2003: 339). Lexical negation is context dependant, as we demonstrate in this section, meaning that specific terms such as long (see example 14) might be positive in certain contexts but are not in others. This justifies our analysing extracts of 400 to 500 words of co-text as opposed to only focusing on concordance lines.

In the extracts analysed in this research, each type of negation is not only present, but is also repeated, rendering it foregrounded by parallelism. Syntactic negation is the most prevalent in the Modernist corpus. When comparing our findings against the British National Corpus (BNC)[6] Written Sample, 'nt' (not abbreviated) is the twenty-eighth keyword featured and has a log-likelihood (LL) of 36.38, indicating statistical significance, as LL values over 15.13 shows a 99.99% level of confidence in the result (Busse et al., 2010; Mahlberg and McIntyre, 2011). Similarly, 'never' is the sixty-fourth keyword of the corpus and has a LL score of 22.67. The BNC is a reference corpus, meaning that it represents 'external norm against which to compare a single text' (McIntyre and Walker, 2019: 26), indicating that syntactic negation occurs more often in the surrounding co-text of *colourless*.

Moreover, morphological negation is also omnipresent in terms surrounding *colourless*, which in itself is a morphologically negated term. Selected examples from our research highlight morphological negation (italics) and lexical negation (underlined):

(11) 'His tranquil *unsuspectingness* of the relativity of his own place in the social scale was probably irritating to M. de Bellegarde, who saw himself reflected in the mind of his potential brother-in-law in a <u>crude</u> and *colorless* form, *unpleasantly dissimilar* to the impressive image projected upon his own intellectual mirror', *The American* (James, 1877).

(12) 'The man, *colourlessly uncouth*, was drinking beer out of a glittering glass; the woman, <u>rustic</u> and <u>placid</u>, leaning back in the <u>rough</u> chair, gazed idly around', *Under Western Eyes* (Conrad, 1911).

(13) 'She had in truth <u>no</u> abstract propensity to <u>malice</u>: she did not *dislike* Lily because the latter was brilliant and predominant, but because she thought that Lily *disliked* her. It is *less* <u>mortifying</u> to believe

---

[6] Available at: www.natcorpox.ac.uk/

one's self *unpopular* than *insignificant*, and vanity prefers to assume that *indifference* is a latent form of *unfriendliness*', *House of Mirth* (Wharton, 1905).

(14) '*Intolerably* <u>monotonous</u> seemed now to the Bunner sisters the treadmill routine of the shop, *colourless* and <u>long</u> their evenings about the lamp, *aimless* their habitual interchange of words to the <u>weary</u> accompaniment of the sewing and pinking machines', *Bunner Sisters* (Wharton, 1916).

(15) 'The Russian woman's way of <u>abolishing</u> the <u>mess</u> and <u>bother</u> of clothes; keeping them close and flat and *untrimmed*. Shining out from them full of <u>dark</u> energy and *indifference*. More <u>oppressively</u> than before, was the <u>barrier</u> between them of Madame Lintoff's *indifference*. It was not <u>hostility</u>. Not personal at all; <u>nor</u> founded on any test, or any opinion. In the *colourless* <u>moaning</u> voice [...] there was an <u>over-whelming</u> *indifference*', *Revolving Lights* (Richardson, 1923).

As the examples illustrate, in the immediate co-text of *colourless*, morphological negation occurs frequently, creating a repetitive structure as *colourless* is in itself negated morphologically. Syntactic negation is also present in each of the analysed extracts, often in the immediate co-text surrounding *colourless*, as shown in example (15). However, lexical negation is the most common form found in the passages.

The repetitive use of negation as a stylistic device could be explained by the term *colourless* being its own opposite, and it can also represent the deprivation of colour, black or darkness, and white or pale. This lack of systematic use, not only between authors but also within extracts by the same author, could be problematic for readers' mental representation of a scene. Indeed, as discussed so far, when *colourless* is used figuratively, it is an image-permitting metaphor (Green, 2017). However, for this to occur, the meaning of the lexeme (dark or pale) must be consistent or an accurate mental representation might not be possible. Thus, the repetition of each type of negation is foregrounded by parallelism because it creates a theme and lexical field, providing readers with a rich mental representation and clarification of what *colourless* entails.

4.2.4 Semantic Associations in Texts Featuring Colourless

Lastly, it is readily apparent the word *colourless* is often joined with other descriptive terms through coordination. The words related through coordinating conjunctions and punctuation are often synonymous or can be considered near-synonyms; these occur in both the attributive and predictive positions. As per the 'parallelism rule', readers are invited to search for connections between parallel structures, coordination, and repetitions (Short, 1996: 14). What is striking is the frequency this occurs, affecting the stylistic composition and leading to a saturation or reinforcement of the notions put forth by the term *colourless*.

In Section 4.2, the literal meaning of *colourless* is provided and contained 'clear' in the definition. However, this word often occurs in the immediate co-text of *colourless* as in the expressions 'colourless, clear complexion', 'clear, colourless, unflinching glance', and 'colourless, clear, glassy dawn'. Similarly, 'colourless' (OED, 2024) is defined as 'lacking bright or conspicuous colour; dull, drab; dim', and 'dull' is linked with the term in the phrase 'the youngest among them was as dull and colourless'. Other near-synonyms related to this definition include 'faint' and 'faded' which occur in the expression 'a scornful grimace as faint and faded and colourless'.

The figurative meaning of 'colourless' (OED, 2024) is 'having no distinctive character, vividness, or intensity; lacking in interest; bland'. Words associated with this definition that are joined with *colourless* in the study texts include 'expressionless', 'flat', and 'eventless'. Similarly, the term 'vague' appears in the expressions: 'His gentle playing was colourless. Vague and woolly' and 'days of wrath dawn upon them colourless and vague'.

The most frequently occurring term joined with colourless is *long*, appearing in phrases such as 'colourless and long their evenings', 'a long, strong, colourless voice', and the parallel construction 'so long, so colourless, so wasted'. Other terms on the scale of dimension include narrow ('longish, narrowish, almost colourless face') and lanky ('colourless, rather lanky hair'). The word *thin* is used alongside *colourless* in two character descriptions: 'thin colourless lips' and 'thin, colourless face'.

The coordinating conjunctions *but* and *yet* also appear in the immediate co-text of *colourless*. The semantic function is to highlight differences in the descriptive terms, as in the contrast between *fresh* and *colourless* in the expressions 'fresh but colourless face' and 'perfectly colourless, yet amazingly fresh'. The effect of coordinators in these expressions is to add to the textual structure by offering contrasting patterns of dissimilar notions. For example, the term colourless is juxtaposed with the abstract concept of space in the phrases 'abundant but rather colorless' and 'spacious but some-what colorless'.

Overall, the frequent semantic association of *colourless* across our corpus with words related to *clear*, *dull*, *faint*, and *vague* is foregrounded by parallelism. This is not only because of the repeated pattern it generates but also because of the synonym-like relation between the terms. This invites readers to perceive *colourless* as having different meanings depending on context, particularly when the immediate co-text provides it through the parallelism rule. It is also worth noting that each parallel term of *colourless* is lexically negated, including the coordinating conjunctions *but* and *yet* as they are used to create contrasting clauses. This reinforces the argument made in Section 4.3 that the omnipresence of negation in the immediate co-text of *colourless* affords readers a rich mental representation of a scene. This is bolstered by the parallel semantic associations described in this section.

4.3 Conclusion

This section investigates the literary and stylistic significance of the lexeme *colourless* in Modernist texts. It employs corpus methods to identify patterns across authors and qualitative analysis of co-text to identify the conceptual roles of the lexeme, revealing the absence of colour is not a neutral concept. The findings challenge this by showing that *colourless* is a predominately negative stylistic marker which can ultimately affect readers' perceptions. Cognitive linguistic tools such as CMT and schemas are used to interpret the observed patterns, revealing that *colourless* is often employed to describe characters and their surroundings and that it is frequently used figuratively, especially to convey characters' physical appearances and personalities. While *colourless* often appears in negative contexts, it also functions in oxymoronic phrases and contrasts with its synonyms, showing that it is not a neutral term despite its literal meaning. These findings shed light on the complex processing and mapping readers undergo when exposed to *colourless* in literary concepts and descriptions.

5 Concluding Remarks

In this Element, we focussed on the relationship between colour, language, cognition, and literature. Our approach followed an interdisciplinary exploration into how colours are perceived and expressed in different linguistic contexts and how they influence cognitive and emotional processes. Through its integration of cognitive linguistics and literary analysis, we aim to provide a comprehensive and holistic understanding of how colour functions within cultural, psychological, and literary frameworks, revealing its multifaceted impact on human perception and interpretation.

A key theme explored in the Element is the linguistic and cultural variability of colour perception. It emphasises that different cultures and languages conceptualise and express colour uniquely, with varying emotional and symbolic meanings attached to colour terms. We have deliberately highlighted this theme in multiple sections, though the degree of emphasis varies depending on the material analysed; this serves as a reminder that colour meanings are not universal but culturally embedded. This variability reflects the culturally embedded nature of colour associations, showing how language shapes emotional and conceptual mappings of colour in everyday communication. The Element highlights that colour-related idioms and expressions differ across cultures, revealing deep connections between language and cultural interpretations of colour.

The cognitive and emotional impact of colours is another significant theme in the Element. It explores how colour perception interacts with cultural schemas to evoke specific emotional and mental responses. Colours are portrayed as carrying emotional significance that transcends mere visual experience, influencing cognitive processing and emotional associations. These colour–emotion links are deeply rooted in both perceptual and cognitive mechanisms and are shaped by cultural contexts, affecting how individuals perceive and interpret their environment.

Furthermore, the symbolic and metaphorical use of colour in literature is also a central focus of the text. The Element discusses how authors employ colour not only as a descriptive element but also as a symbolic device to convey deeper meanings. By mirroring cultural configurations, authors use colours to reflect characters' emotions, traits, or thematic elements within narratives, creating layers of meaning that extend beyond the visual description. Through this symbolic use, colours serve as powerful metaphors that enhance readers' engagement with literary texts and their underlying themes.

The Element also examines how colours are frequently used to reflect moral or emotional qualities in literature, reinforcing narrative development and character portrayal. By associating specific colours with character attributes, the text demonstrates how visual cues contribute to shaping readers' perceptions of literary characters and their internal states. Finally, we engaged with psychological research through the lens of metaphor theory to show how colour associations are ingrained in both linguistic and cognitive processes. It argues that certain colour metaphors are deeply embedded in human cognition, shaping how people understand and interpret various concepts. These metaphors, which are pervasive across cultures, reflect not only linguistic conventions but also cognitive patterns that influence perception and meaning-making.

Throughout the Element, we have also sought to provide a systematic approach that can guide further research. While we do not claim a fully generalisable framework, our integration of literary analysis, cognitive–linguistic mappings, corpus methods, and psychological findings demonstrates a methodical way to study colour in literary contexts. Researchers could adopt or adapt this approach to explore other texts, languages, or cultural contexts.

Overall, through its focus on linguistic variability, emotional and cognitive impacts, and metaphor theory, the Element provides a thorough and insightful analysis of how colour shapes cultures, human perception, and literary interpretation. This Element not only fills a gap in existing research but also opens new avenues for interdisciplinary studies. We are careful to note that while some findings reflect prior research, this Element's contribution lies in showing how these insights can be combined systematically to illuminate colour's role in literature. By combining insights from cognitive linguistics, psychology, and literary criticism, this Element provides a new framework for understanding how colours function in literature and not just as elements of description, but as essential components of how we perceive, process, and experience the world. The innovative nature of this work lies in its holistic, cross-disciplinary approach, which deepens our understanding of the complex roles that colours play in both cognitive processes and literary expressions.

References

'black, adj. and n.'. *OED Online*. March 2024. Oxford University Press. Available at: www-oed-com.libaccess.hud.ac.uk/view/Entry/19670?rskey=fILY37&result=1 (04 April 2022).

'colour or color, n.1'. *OED Online*. March 2024. Oxford University Press. Available at: www-oed-com.libaccess.hud.ac.uk/view/Entry/36596?rskey=EwHtDN&result=1&isAdvanced=false (04 April 2022).

'colourless or colorless, adj.'. *OED Online*. March 2024. Oxford University Press. Available at: www-oed-com.libaccess.hud.ac.uk/view/Entry/36617?redirectedFrom=colourless (04 April 2022).

'white, adj. (and adv.) and n.'. *OED Online*. March 2024. Oxford University Press. Available at: www-oed-com.libaccess.hud.ac.uk/view/Entry/228566?rskey=q8cBfB&result=1&isAdvanced=false (04 April 2022).

Abrams, M. H., & Harpham, G. G. 2005. *A glossary of literary terms* (8th ed). Stamford: Thomson.

Alter, A., Stern, C., Granot, Y., & Balcetis, E. 2016. The 'Bad Is Black' effect: Why people believe evildoers have darker skin than do-gooders. *Personality and Social Psychology Bulletin, 42*(12), 1653–1665.

Althubaiti, T. S. 2015. Race discourse in Wuthering Heights. *European Scientific Journal, 11*(8), 201–225.

Ammons, E. 1980. *Edith Wharton's argument with America*. Athens: University of Georgia Press.

Anderson, A. A. 2021. Imagery and how it works in Lorca's Poeta en Nueva York: The case of '1910 (Intermedio)'. *Forum for Modern Language Studies 57*(1), 1–20.

Anwer, R. 2023. 'Painting with words': Color terminology and pragmatic resonance in Alice Walker's The color purple (1982). *Research Journal in Advanced Humanities, 4*(3), 165–183.

Arnheim, R. 1969. *Art and visual perception*. London: Faber and Faber.

Baker, S. 2004. 'Colour and emotion in design', in McDonagh, D., Hekkert, P., van Erp, J., & Gyi, D. (eds.), *Design and emotion*. London: Taylor & Francis, 188–192.

Bartlett, F. C. 1995. *Remembering: A study in experimental and social psychology*. Cambridge: Cambridge University Press.

Baylis, P., Obradovich, N., Kryvasheyeu, Y., Chen, H., Coviello, L., Moro, E., Cebrian, M., & Fowler, J. H. 2018. Weather impacts expressed sentiment. *PLoS One, 13*(4), e0195750.

Bennetts, L. 1978, July 7. Supporters of the Equal Rights Amendment gathering for march in Washington Sunday. *The New York Times*. Available at: www.nytimes.com/1978/07/07/archives/supporters-of-the-equal-rights-amendment-gathering-for-march-in.html

Berlin, B., & Kay, P. 1969. *Basic color terms: Their universality and evolution*. Berkeley: University of California Press.

Biggam, C. P., & Kay, C. J. (eds.). 2006. *Progress in colour studies: Volume I. Language and culture*. Amsterdam: John Benjamins.

Biggam, C. P., Hough, C. A., Kay, C. J., & Simmons, D. R. (eds.). 2011. *New directions in colour studies*. Amsterdam: John Benjamins.

Boerger, M. A. 2005. Variations in figurative language use as a function of mode of communication. *Journal of Psycholinguistic Research*, *34*(1), 31–49.

Brontë, C. 1847/2007. Jane Eyre. *Project Gutenberg*. Available at: gutenberg.org/files/1260/1260-h/1260-h.htm (26 March 2022).

Brontë, C. 1849/2024. Shirley. *Project Gutenberg*. Available at: www.gutenberg.org/files/30486/30486-h/30486-h.htm

Brontë, E. 1847/2021. Wuthering Heights. *Project Gutenberg*. Available at: www.gutenberg.org/files/768/768-h/768-h.htm (26 March 2022).

Burriss, L., & McComb, D. 2001. Use of color in three news magazines to identify political parties. *Journal of Visual Literacy*, *21*(2), 167–176.

Busse, B., McIntyre, D., Nørgaard, N., & Toolan, M. 2010. John McGahern's stylistic and narratological art. *Journal in English Lexicology*, *5*, 101–131.

Butt, D. G., & Lukin, A. 2009. Stylistic analysis: Construing aesthetic organisation, in Halliday, M. A. K., & Webster, J. J (eds.), *Continuum companion to systemic functional linguistics*. London: Continuum, 190–215.

Callahan, A. 2003. Eye to eye: Painting white whale: Moby Dick I. *Leviathan*, *5*(1), 52–57.

Carroll, N. 1996. The paradox of suspense, in Vorderer, P., Wulff, H. J., & Friedrichsen, M. (eds.), *Suspense: Conceptualizations, theoretical analyses, and empirical explorations*. London: Routledge, 147–188.

Childs, P. 2008. *Modernism*. Milton: Routledge.

Chomsky, N. 1956. Three models for the description of language. *IRE Transactions on Information Theory*, *2*(3), 113–124.

Cook, G. W. D. 1990. A theory of discourse deviation: The application of schema theory to the analysis of literary discourse (Doctoral dissertation, The University of Leeds).

Cross, M., & Berger, K. S. 1993. *Henry James: The contingencies of style.* New York: Springer.

Cunningham, M. R. 1979. Weather, mood, and helping behavior: Quasi experiments with the sunshine samaritan. *Journal of Personality and Social Psychology, 37*(11), 1947–1956.

Dael, N., Perseguers, M. N., Marchand, C., Antonietti, J. P., & Mohr, C. 2016. Put on that colour, it fits your emotion: Colour appropriateness as a function of expressed emotion. *Quarterly Journal of Experimental Psychology, 9*(8), 1619–1630.

Dancygier, B. 2014. Intensity and texture in imagery, in Stockwell, P., & Whiteley, S. (eds.), *The Cambridge handbook of stylistics.* Cambridge: Cambridge University Press, 212–228.

De la Ramée, L. 1867/2024. Under two flags. Project Gutenberg. Available at: www.gutenberg.org/files/3465/3465-h/3465-h.htm

Dedrick, D. 1998. *Naming the rainbow: Colour language, colour science, and culture: 274.* Berlin: Springer Science & Business Media.

Department for Education. 2013a. *English language GCSE subject content and assessment objectives.* Available at:assets.publishing.service.gov.uk/government/uploads/system/uploads/attachment_data/file/254497/GCSE_English_language.pdf (26 March 2022).

Department for Education. 2013b. *English literature GCSE subject content and assessment objectives.* Available at: assets.publishing.service.gov.uk/government/uploads/system/uploads/attachment_data/file/254498/GCSE_English_literature.pdf (26 March 2022).

DorothyRichardson.org. 2025. *Dorothy Richardson: Biography.* Available at: www.dorothyrichardson.org/biography.htm

Drewery, C. 2016. *Modernist short fiction by women: The liminal in Katherine Mansfield, Dorothy Richardson, May Sinclair and Virginia Woolf.* Milton: Routledge.

Edwards, B. 2004. *Color: A course in mastering the art of mixing colors.* New York: Penguin.

Elliot, A., & Maier, M. 2014. Color psychology: Effects of perceiving color on psychological functioning in humans. *Annual Review of Psychology, 65*, 95–120.

Finke, R. A. 1989. *Principles of mental imagery.* Cambridge, MA: The Massachusetts Institute of Technology Press.

Flaubert, G. 1857/2021. Madame Bovary. Project Gutenberg. Available at: www.gutenberg.org/files/2413/2413-h/2413-h.htm (26 March 2022).

Forceville, C., & Renckens, T. 2013. The good is light and bad is dark metaphor in feature films. *Metaphor and the Social World, 3*(2), 160–179.

Frost, L. 2002. Dorothy Richardson, in Janik, V. K., & Janik, D. I. (eds.), *Modern British women writers: An A-to-Z*. London: Greenwood Press, 173–179.

Giovanelli, M. 2013. *Text world theory and Keats' poetry: The cognitive poetics of desire, dreams and nightmares*. London: Bloomsbury Academic.

Graham, K. 1996. Conradian narrative, in Stape, J. H. (ed.), *The Cambridge companion to Joseph Conrad*. Cambridge: Cambridge University Press, 160–178.

Grandjean, E. 1973. *Ergonomics of the home*. Translated by H. Oldroyd. London: Taylor and Francis.

Green, M. 2017. Imagery, expression, and metaphor. *Philosophical Studies*, *174*, 33–46.

Halpern, A. R. 1988. Mental scanning in auditory imagery for songs. *Journal of Experimental Psychology: Learning, Memory, and Cognition*, *14*(3), 434–443.

Haytock, J. 2008. *Edith Wharton and the conversations of literary modernism*. New York: Palgrave.

Herman, D. 2001. Style-shifting in Edith Wharton's *The house of mirth*. *Language and Literature*, *10*(1), 61–77.

Hidalgo-Downing, L. 2000a. Negation in discourse: A text world approach to Joseph Heller's Catch-22. *Language and Literature*, *9*(3), 215–239.

Hidalgo-Downing, L. 2000b. *Negation, text worlds, and discourse: The pragmatics of fiction (No. 66)*. Santa Barbara: Greenwood Publishing Group.

Hidalgo-Downing, L. 2003. Negation as a stylistic feature in Joseph Heller's Catch-22: A corpus study. *Style*, *37*(3), 318–340.

Hill, S. 1983/2011. *The woman in Black*. London: Vintage Classics.

Howarth, E., & Hoffman, M. 1984. A multidimensional approach to the relationship between mood and weather. *British Journal of Psychology*, *75*(1), 15–23.

HUM19UK, Version 1. 2019. University of Huddersfield, Utrecht University, University College Roosevelt, Middelburg. Available at:www.linguisticsathuddersfield.com/hum19uk-corpus (23 March 2022).

Hupka, R. B., Zaleski, Z., Otto, J., Reidl, L., & Tarabrina, N. V. 1997. The colors of anger, envy, fear, and jealousy: A cross-cultural study. *Journal of Cross-Cultural Psychology*, *28*(2), 156–171.

Imsallim, W. M. 2014. Symbolism and imagery in Emily Bronte's Wuthering Heights (Master dissertation, University of Benghazi, Libya).

Iwata, Y. 2009. Creating suspense and surprise in short literary fiction: A stylistic and narratological approach (Doctoral dissertation, University of Birmingham, UK).

Joao Cordeiro, M. 2015. The colour blue: Perceptions and representations in travel and tourism, in Bogushevskaya, V., & Colla, E. (eds.), *Thinking colours: Perception, translation and representation*. Cambridge: Cambridge Scholars Publishing, 206–225.

Jonauskaite, D., Wicker, J., Mohr, C., Dael, N., Havelka, J., Papadatou-Pastou, M., Zhang, M., & Oberfeld, D. 2019. A machine learning approach to quantify the specificity of colour–emotion associations and their cultural differences. *Royal Society Open Science*, 6: 1907412, 1–19.

Jonauskaite, D., Abu-Akel, A., Dael, N., Oberfeld, D., Abdel-Khalek, A. M., Al-Rasheed, A. S., Antonietti, J.-P., Bogushevskaya, V., Chamseddine, A., Chkonia, E., Corona, V., Fonseca-Pedrero, E., Griber, Y. A., Grimshaw, G., Hasan, A. A., Havelka, J., Hirnstein, M., Karlsson, B. S. A., Laurent, E., Lindeman, M., Marquardt, L., Mefoh, P., Papadatou-Pastou, M., Pérez-Albéniz, A., Pouyan, N., Roinishvili, M., Romanyuk, L., Salgado Montejo, A., Schrag, Y., Sultanova, A., Uusküla, M., Vainio, S., Wąsowicz, G., Zdravković, S., Zhang, M., & Mohr, C. 2020a. Universal patterns in color-emotion associations are further shaped by linguistic and geographic proximity. *Psychological Science*, *31*(10), 1245–1260.

Jonauskaite, D., Parraga, C. A., Quiblier, M., & Mohr, C. 2020b. Feeling blue or seeing red? Similar patterns of emotion associations with colour patches and colour terms. *i-Perception*, *11*(1), 1–24.

Kaskatayeva, Z. A., Mazhitayeva, S., Omasheva, Z. M., Nygmetova, N., & Kadyrov, Z. 2020. Colour categories in different linguistic cultures. *Rupkatha Journal on Interdisciplinary Studies in Humanities*, *12*(6), 1–13.

Kay, P., Berlin, B., & Merrifield, W. 1991. Biocultural implications of systems of color naming. *Journal of Linguistic Anthropology*, *1*(1), 12–25.

Kha, H. N. M., & Nhung, L. T. H. 2024. Symbolism of the color white in Jane Austen's works. *Journal of Science and Technology*, *22*(9b), 43–48.

Knapp, J. P. 1980. *Madame Bovary: The dialectics of color and light* (Doctoral dissertation, The University of Arizona).

Koller, V. 2008. 'Not just a colour': Pink as a gender and sexuality marker in visual communication. *Visual Communication*, *7*(4), 395–423.

References

Kövecses, Z. 2002. *Metaphor: A practical introduction*. Oxford: Oxford University Press.

Kövecses, Z. 2008. Metaphor and emotion, in Gibbs, R. (ed.), *The Cambridge handbook of metaphor and thought*. Cambridge: Cambridge University Press, 380–396.

Krafts, K. P., Hempelmann, E., & Oleksyn, B. J. 2011. The color purple: From royalty to laboratory, with apologies to Malachowski. *Biotechnic & Histochemistry*, *86*(1), 7–35.

Kuiken, D., Miall, D. S., & Sikora, S. 2004. Forms of self-implication in literary reading. *Poetics Today*, *25*(2), 171–203.

Kumarasamy, J., Devi Apayee, P., & Subramaniam, M. 2014. Emotion and expression responses through colour: A literature review. *SSRN*, 1–13. Available at: https://doi.org/10.2139/ssrn.2435741.

Lakoff, G., & Johnson, M. 1980. *Metaphors we live by*. Chicago, IL: The University of Chicago Press.

Lakoff, G., & Turner, M. 1989. *More than cool reason: A field guide to poetic metaphor*. Chicago & London: The University of Chicago Press.

Lakoff, G., Espenson, J., & Schwartz, A. 1991. *Master metaphor list*. (Draft 2nd ed.) Berkeley: Cognitive Linguistics Group, University of California at Berkeley.

Le Fanu, D. 2003. Black and White in *Wuthering Heights* the etchings of Rosalind Whitman. *Brontë Studies*, *28*(3), 237–246.

Leech, G. 1983. *The Principles of pragmatics*. London: Longman.

Leech, G. 2008. *Language of literature: Style and foregrounding*. London & New York: Routledge.

Leech, G., & Short, M. 2007. *Style in fiction: A linguistic introduction to English fictional prose* (2nd ed.). Harlow: Pearson Longman.

Loreto, V., Mukherjee, A., & Tria, F. 2012. On the origin of the hierarchy of colour names. *Psychological and Cognitive Sciences*, *109*(18), 6819–6824.

Lothe, J. 1996. Conrad and Modernism, in Stape, J. H. (ed.), *The Cambridge Companion to Joseph Conrad*. Cambridge: Cambridge University Press, 203–222.

Mahlberg, M. 2009. Corpus Stylistics and the Pickwickian watering-pot, in Baker, P. (ed.), *Contemporary corpus linguistics*. London: Continuum International Publishing Group, 47–63.

Mahlberg, M., & McIntyre, D. 2011. A case for corpus stylistics: Ian Fleming's Casino Royale. *English Text Construction*, *4*(2), 204–227.

Mahlberg, M., & Smith, C. 2010. Corpus approaches to prose fiction: Civility and body language in *Pride and Prejudice*, in McIntyre, D. & Busse, B. (eds.), *Language and style*. Basingstoke: Palgrave Macmillan, 449–467.

Mahlberg, M., Stockwell, P., Wiegand, V., & Lentin, J. 2020. *CLiC 2.1. Corpus Linguistics in Context.* Available at: https://clic.bham.ac.uk/ (4 April 2022).

Mahnke, F. 1996. *Color, environment and human response*. New York: John Wiley.

Martin, J. R., & White P. R. R. 2005. *The language of valuation: Appraisal in English*. New York: Palgrave Macmillan.

McClure, S., & Pager-McClymont, K. 2022. *The Modernist Literature Project*. Available at: https://modernistliteratureproject.org/

McIntyre, D., & Walker, B. 2019. *Corpus stylistics: Theory and practice*. Edinburgh: Edinburgh University Press.

Meier, B., & Robinson, M. 2005. The metaphorical representation of affect. *Metaphor and Symbol*, *20*, 239–257.

Melville, H. 1851/1988. *Moby-Dick or, the whale*. New York: Penguin.

Miall, D. S., & Kuiken, D. 1994. Foregrounding, defamiliarization, and affect: Response to literary stories. *Poetics*, *22*(5), 389–407.

Mohr, C., Jonauskaite, D., Dan-Glauser, E. S., Uusküla, M., & Dael, N. 2018. Unifying research on colour and emotion: Time for a cross-cultural survey on emotion associations with colour terms, in MacDonald, L., Biggam, C. P. & Paramei, G. V. (eds.), *Progress in colour studies: Cognition, language and beyond*. Amsterdam: John Benjamins Publishing Company, 209–222.

Mukařovský, J. 1932/1964. Standard language and poetic language, in Garvin, L. (ed.), *A Prague school reader on aesthetics, literary structure, and style*. Washington, DC: Georgetown University Press, 17–30.

Nanay, B. 2015. Perceptual content and the content of mental imagery. *Philosophical Studies*, *172*, 1723–1736.

Nanay, B. 2017. Sensory substitution and multimodal mental imagery. *Perception*, *46*(9), 1014–1026

Nanay, B. 2018. Multimodal mental imagery. *Cortex*, *105*, 125–134.

Nørgaard, N. 2007. Disordered collarettes and uncovered tables: Negative polarity as a stylistic device in Joyce's 'Two gallants'. *Journal of Literary Semantics*, *36*(1), 35–52.

O'Connor, Z. 2011. Colour psychology and colour therapy: Caveat emptor. *Color Research & Application*, *36*(3), 229–234.

References

Pager-McClymont, K. 2021a. *Communicating Emotions through Surroundings: A Stylistic Model of Pathetic Fallacy* (Doctoral Dissertation, University of Huddersfield, UK).

Pager-McClymont, K. 2021b. Introducing Jane: The power of the opening, in Pöhls, V., & Utudji, M. (eds.), *Powerful prose: How textual features impact readers*. Bielefeld: Transcript Lettre, 111–127.

Pager-McClymont, K. 2022. 'Linking emotions to surroundings: A stylistic model of pathetic fallacy'. *Language and Literature*. Available at: https://doi.org/10.1177/09639470221106021

Pager-McClymont, K. 2023. "The thunder rolls and the lightning strikes": Pathetic fallacy as a multimodal metaphor. *Anglica Wratislaviensia*, *61*(1), 53–75.

Palmer, S. E., & Schloss, K. B. 2010. An ecological valence theory of human color preference. *Proceedings of the National Academy of Sciences*, *107*(19), 8877–8882.

Parsons, D. 2014. *Theorists of the Modernist novel: James Joyce, Dorothy Richardson and Virginia Woolf*. Milton: Routledge.

Persinger, M. 1975. Lag response in mood reports to changes in the weather matrix. *International Journal of Biometeorology*, *19*(2), 108–114.

Plevíková, I. 2016. Lolita: A cultural analysis (Master's Dissertation, Masaryk University, Czech Republic).

Pollard, P. 1981. Colour symbolism in 'Le Rouge et le Noir'. *The Modern Language Review*, *76*(2), 323–331.

Prado-León, L. R., Avilla-Chaurand, R., & Rosales-Cinco, R. A. 2006. Colour associations in the Mexican university population, in Biggam, C., & Kay, C. J. (eds.), *Progress in colour studies: Psychological aspects*. Amsterdam: John Benjamins, 189–202.

Prado-León, L. R., Schloss, K. B., & Palmer, S. E. 2014. Color, music, and emotion in Mexican and US populations. New Directions in Colour Studies. Amsterdam: John Benjamins.

Rayson, P. 2009. Wmatrix: A web-based corpus processing environment, Computing Department, Lancaster University. Available at: http://ucrel.lancs.ac.uk/wmatrix/

Redden, M. S. 2011. Moby-Dick and the color of the elusive. *Apollon*, *1*, 4–9.

Ruskin, J. 1856/2012. Modern painters Vol. III. *Project Gutenberg*. Available at: gutenberg.org/files/38923/38923-h/38923-h.htm (26 March 2022).

Sandford, J. 2011. Warm, cool, light, dark, or afterimage: Dimensions and connotations of conceptual color metaphor/metonym, in Biggam, C., Hough, C. A., Kay, C. J., & Simmons, D. R. (eds.), *New directions in colour studies*. Amsterdam: John Benjamins, 205–218.

Sartre, J-P. 1974. *Between existentialism and marxism*. London: New Left Books.

Saxbe, D. E., & Repetti, R. 2010. No place like home: Home tours correlate with daily patterns of mood and cortisol. *Personality and Social Psychology Bulletin*, *36*(1), 71–81.

Shakespeare, W. 1606/2014. *Macbeth*. Minneapolis, MN: First Avenue Editions.

Shinohara, K., & Matsunaka, Y. 2009. Pictorial metaphors of emotion in Japanese comics, in Forceville, C., & Urios-Aparisi, E. (eds.), *Multimodal metaphor*. Berlin: Mouton de Gruyter, 265–293.

Short, M. 1996. *Exploring the language of poems, plays, and prose*. London: Longman.

Simon, L. 2007. *The critical reception of Henry James: Creating a master*. Rochester, NY: Camden House.

Simpson, P. 2014. *Stylistics: A resource book for students*. London: Routledge.

Soberano, E. 2023. Heathcliff as bog creature: Racialized ecologies in Wuthering Heights. *Nineteenth-Century Contexts*, *45*(2), 145–164.

Soriano, C., & Valenzuela, J. 2009. Emotion and colour across languages: Implicit associations in Spanish colour terms. *Social Science Information*, *48*(3), 421–445.

Sotirova, V. 2013. *Consciousness in modernist fiction: A stylistic study*. Basingstoke: Palgrave Macmillan.

Stendhal. 1830/2020. Le Rouge et le Noir. *Project Gutenberg*. Available at: www.gutenberg.org/cache/epub/798/pg798-images.html (26 March 2022).

Stevenson, R. L. 1886/2018. The Strange Case of Dr. *Jekyll And Mr. Hyde*. *Project Gutenberg*. Available at: gutenberg.org/files/43/43-h/43-h.htm (26 March 2022).

Stockwell, P. 1999. The inflexibility of invariance. *Language and Literature*, *8*(2), 125–142.

Stockwell, P. 2014. Atmosphere and tone, in Stockwell, P., & Whiteley, S. (eds.), *The Cambridge handbook of stylistics*. Cambridge: Cambridge University Press, 360–374.

Stoker, B. 1897/2013. Dracula. *Project Gutenberg*. Available at: gutenberg.org/files/345/345-h/345-h.htm (26 March 2022).

Stoll, E. E. 1951. Symbolism in Moby-Dick. *Journal of the History of Ideas, 12*(4), 440–465.

Sutton, T., & Altarriba, J. 2016. Color associations to emotion and emotion-laden words: A collection of norms for stimulus construction and selection. *Behavior Research Methods, 48*(2), 686–728.

The British National Corpus, version 3 (BNC XML Edition). 2007. Distributed by Bodleian Libraries, University of Oxford, on behalf of the BNC Consortium. Available at: www.natcorpox.ac.uk/ (05 April 2022).

Tipper, P. A. 1989. *Colour symbolism in the works of Gustave Flaubert* (Doctoral dissertation, University of Hull).

Tottie, G. 1991. *Negation in English speech and writing: A study in variation.* San Diego, CA: San Diego Academic Press.

Valdez, P., & Mehrabian, A. 1994. Effects of color on emotions. *Journal of Experimental Psychology: General, 123*(4), 394–409.

van Peer, W. 2007. Introduction to foregrounding: A state of the art. *Language and Literature 16*(2), 99–104.

Wales, K. 2011. *A dictionary of stylistics* (3rd ed.). Harlow: Pearson Longman.

Walker, A. 1982. *The color purple.* Boston, MA: Houghton Mifflin Harcourt.

Wang, T., Shu, S., & Mo, L. 2014. Blue or red? The effects of colour on the emotions of Chinese people. *Asian Journal of Social Psychology, 17*(2), 152–158.

Ward, M. A. 1888/2021. Robert Elsmere. *Project Gutenberg.* Available at: www.gutenberg.org/cache/epub/24898/pg24898-images.html

Ware, M. S. 2004. The architecture of the short story: Edith Wharton's Modernist practice. *Edith Wharton Review, 20*(2), 17–23.

Watanabe, H. 1962. Past perfect retrospection in the style of Henry James. *American Literature, 34*(2), 165–181.

Wu, Z., & Wei, L. 2022. A study on symbolic connotations and metaphorical implications in 'The Color Purple'. *Advances in Literary Study, 10*(2), 224–233.

Yildirim, K., Akalin-Baskaya, A., & Hidayetoglu, M. L. 2007. Effects of indoor color on mood and cognitive performance. *Building and Environment, 42*(9), 3233–3240.

Cambridge Elements

Cognitive Linguistics

Sarah Duffy
Northumbria University

Sarah Duffy is Senior Lecturer in English Language and Linguistics at Northumbria University. She has published primarily on metaphor interpretation and understanding, and her forthcoming monograph for Cambridge University Press (co-authored with Michele Feist) explores *Time, Metaphor, and Language* from a cognitive science perspective. Sarah is Review Editor of the journal, *Language and Cognition*, and Vice President of the UK Cognitive Linguistics Association.

Nick Riches
Newcastle University

Nick Riches is a Senior Lecturer in Speech and Language Pathology at Newcastle University. His work has investigated language and cognitive processes in children and adolescents with autism and developmental language disorders, and he is particularly interested in usage-based accounts of these populations.

Editorial Board

Heng Li, *Southwest University*
John Newman, *University of Alberta (Edmonton)*
Kimberley Pager-McClymont, *University of Huddersfield*
Katie J. Patterson, *Universidad de Granada*
Maria Angeles Ruiz-Moneva, *University of Zaragoza*
Lexi Webster, *Manchester Metropolitan University*
Xu Wen, *Southwest University*

About the Series

Cambridge Elements in Cognitive Linguistics aims to extend the theoretical and methodological boundaries of cognitive linguistics. It will advance and develop established areas of research in the discipline, as well as address areas where it has not traditionally been explored and areas where it has yet to become well-established.

Cambridge Elements

Cognitive Linguistics

Elements in the Series

Language Change and Cognitive Linguistics: Case Studies from the History of Russian
Tore Nesset

Navigating the Realities of Metaphor and Psychotherapy Research
Dennis Tay

The Many Faces of Creativity: Exploring Synaesthesia through a Metaphorical Lens Sarah Turner and Jeannette Littlemore

Metaphor, Metonymy, the Body and the Environment: An Exploration of the Factors That Shape Emotion-Colour Associations and Their Variation across Cultures
Jeannette Littlemore, Marianna Bolognesi, Nina Julich-Warpakowski, Chung-hong Danny Leung and Paula Pérez Sobrino

Applied Cognitive Linguistics and L2 Instruction
Reyes Llopis-García

Cognitive Linguistics and Language Evolution
Michael Pleyer and Stefan Hartmann

Computational Construction Grammar: A Usage-Based Approach
Jonathan Dunn

Signed Language and Cognitive Grammar
Sherman Wilcox, Rocío Martínez, and Sara Siyavoshi

Linguistic Synesthesia: A Meta-analysis
Bodo Winter and Francesca Strik-Lievers

Cognition and Conspiracy Theories
Andreas Musolff

Creative Construction Grammar
Thomas Hoffmann and Mark Turner

Colour Concepts from a Linguistic and Literary Perspective
Kimberley Pager-McClymont, Suzanne McClure, and Amélie Doche

A full series listing is available at: www.cambridge.org/ECOG

For EU product safety concerns, contact us at Calle de José Abascal, 56–1°,
28003 Madrid, Spain or eugpsr@cambridge.org.

www.ingramcontent.com/pod-product-compliance
Lightning Source LLC
LaVergne TN
LVHW020006080526
838200LV00081B/4409